CHICKEN
FOR DINNER
AND MUCH, MUCH MORE

Author: Annette Wolter

Photography: Susi and Pete A. Eising

Translated by UPS Translations, London

Edited by Josephine Bacon

CLB 4181
This edition published in 1996 by Colour Library Direct
Published originally under the title "Geflügel" by Gräfe
und Unzer Verlag GmbH, München
© 1995 Gräfe und Unzer Verlag GmbH, München
English translation copyright: © 1996 by
CLB International, Godalming, Surrey
Typeset by Image Setting, Brighton, E. Sussex
Printed and bound in Singapore
ISBN 1-85833-320-2

CHICKEN
FOR DINNER
AND MUCH, MUCH MORE

Annette Wolter

Contributors
Elke Alsen, Marieluise Christl-Licosa,
Marey Kurz, Hannelore Mähl-Strenge,
Annedore Meineke, Brigitta Stuber,
Renate Zelter and Annette Wolter

Photography
Susi and Pete A. Eising

Colour
Library

Contents

Dishes for Special Occasions

Delicious Stuffings

Cold Poultry Cuisine

Useful Information about Poultry

Index

About this Book

From both a culinary and a nutritional point of view, fresh poultry cannot be praised enough: it is easy to digest, high in protein and relatively economical, offering a multitude of dishes for everyday cooking and special occasions.

As you leaf through this book, you will be tempted to try out the huge range of recipes, including many tips and variations. The instructions are so straightforward and easy to follow that cooking becomes a pleasure – even for inexperienced cooks.

This splendidly illustrated cookery book contains favourite recipes from all over the world, and is a magnificent demonstration of the sheer versatility of poultry. The 150 recipes are illustrated with superb colour photographs, taken especially for this book. Our recipes and your cooking skills prove just how tasty good, fresh, properly kept poultry can be – particularly when correctly prepared.

Introductions to each recipe indicate whether, for example, the dish is a famous regional dish, a national speciality or a wholefood recipe. Instantly accessible facts on preparation and cooking times, as well as the kilojoule, kilocalorie, protein, fat and carbohydrate contents make it easier for you to plan a nutritious meal.

The recipes are divided into four substantial chapters. The first of these is 'Delicious Soups and Hearty Stews' – with something to suit all tastes from a delicate consommé to a satisfying pot-au-feu. The second chapter is devoted to 'Braised Dishes and Ragouts'. You will love Braised Herb Chicken or Duckling with Tomatoes, not to mention classics such as Chicken Marengo. This section is followed by 'Dishes for Special Occasions', including many ideas for entertaining. Pheasant with Bacon Sauce, Partridge with Savoy Cabbage and Stuffed Guinea Fowl will appeal to even the most discerning gourmet. 'Cold Poultry Cuisine' contains many recipes for parties and cold buffets, such as Turkey Mousse with Two Sauces and Chicken Salad with Oranges. Many of the recipes are also excellent for Sunday brunches or picnics.

Finally, our book also contains a good selection of specially tried and tested tasty stuffings for poultry.

Other invaluable parts of the book include colour, step-by-step photographs of important preparatory stages: drawing, jointing, perfect stuffing and the correct method of trussing and larding. There is also detailed information on the most common cooking methods, such as spit-roasting, poaching, roasting in cooking foil and on a grid, and braising, as well as instructions for carving poultry. An easy-to-read, fully illustrated summary of the poultry types mentioned in the book contains important information. The book also provides an extensive table of cooking times for the individual birds, using various cooking methods and, where appropriate, the settings for electric, fan-assisted and gas ovens.

The recipes have been selected from a range of tried and tested favourites, successful recipes from our team of authors and from our personal associations with particular regions or countries. Of course, an awareness of modern nutrition and a respect for the discerning palate also determined which recipes were included. You will, therefore, find specialities from many countries: America, France, Britain, Spain, Russia and the Netherlands. Among the most popular recipes, we include Coq au Vin, Creamed Chicken and Chicken Soufflé. Traditional recipes for pheasant, guinea fowl, partridge, pigeon, quail and wild duck are also included.

Before you start on your first poultry dish, after browsing through the tempting and delicious recipes, please read the important section on buying poultry.

Have fun buying, cooking and eating your poultry.

Unless stated otherwise, all the recipes are designed to serve 4 people. KJ and kcal stand for kilojoules and kilocalories.

Buying Poultry

When buying poultry, it is worth bearing in mind a few important quality characteristics, since even birds offered for sale as 'premium goods' should be critically inspected. Obviously, the way in which the poultry is to be used plays a role in its selection.

If you want to make a strong stock, a large chicken is just the right thing: it provides a rich flavour. Once the stock has cooled down, the fat can easily be removed. The remaining stock can be rubbed through a sieve and thickened by boiling in an uncovered saucepan before using. Alternatively, rub the stock through a sieve and freeze in an ice-cube tray. The cubes can be used as required for soups and sauces, and stored in the freezer for up to 6 months. The lean chicken joints can be used in soufflés and salads. An even more economical stock can be obtained from using frozen poultry offal.

You can choose from a wide range of fresh and frozen poultry. Corn-fed chickens, large chickens and 'super' chickens, corn-fed ducks, geese, turkeys and prepared poultry portions, such as thighs, breasts and rolled joints, are on sale. It can be assumed that frozen poultry and game has been slaughtered, packaged and quick-frozen under impeccably hygienic conditions. Although transport by refrigerated lorry does not lead to any loss of quality, transfer, interim storage or improper handling in the retail trade can result in a poorer product. Therefore, it is sensible to buy frozen poultry and game only from retailers' freezers which are not heavily iced and where the goods are not stacked above the visible maximum load line. Always read what is printed on the

packaging! The approximate age of the bird can be estimated from its weight and description. The 'sell by' date is also shown. Always make sure that the packaging is not damaged and

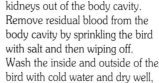

that the skin is an even colour. Dark patches, leaking blood and ice crystals in the packaging indicate that the bird has been incorrectly handled and its quality will have been affected.

It is easy to test the age and quality of fresh poultry that has not yet been prepared for cooking: young, healthy birds have a flexible breastbone, strong feet and taught, elastic skin on the legs, sharp claws that have not yet worn away and, sometimes, a bright red comb. The skin shows no partial discolouration, bruising or other injury. Cloudy, sunken eyes, streaky or irregularly discoloured skin, together with changes in smell, indicate poultry or game that is old or has been poorly stored.

Before cooking fresh game birds, in particular, you must check carefully whether it has been correctly and thoroughly drawn. Any remaining feathers or quills can be plucked out with tweezers or singed (see page 8). Remove any remaining lung tissue from the backbone and take the

kidneys out of the body cavity. Remove residual blood from the body cavity by sprinkling the bird with salt and then wiping off. Wash the inside and outside of the bird with cold water and dry well, since bacteria thrive in a damp environment.

Very young poultry that has not developed a full flavour can be marinated. You can rub the bird with seasoned oil or place it in a marinade for several hours. Dry the bird before roasting or grilling. Use seasoned oil for basting during cooking; a liquid marinade can be used for braising or for preparing a sauce. Take care when using mixtures of seasoning that you have invented yourself; it is usually best to use a tried and tested recipe. Marinades usually consist of wine, sherry, mixtures of water and wine vinegar or lemon juice, onion, herbs, paprika, pepper and cloves, ginger or garlic. It is important to omit salt from the marinade, as it may cause the meat to dry out slightly and turn the skin leathery.

Fresh poultry should not be stored for more than 2 days in the refrigerator. Frozen poultry can be stored for up to 6 months. If you wish to freeze prepared poultry dishes, you should observe a few rules:

● Do not overcook the meat before freezing, as it will cook further when it is reheated.
● Use herbs sparingly before freezing; garlic, nutmeg, cloves, pepper and onions increase in flavour as a result of the freezing process.
● Sauces are best thickened with cream or egg yolk after defrosting and reheating rather than before.
● If possible, add vegetable ingredients to the hot dish after freezing.

Cooking Poultry

Cleaning and Drawing Poultry

If you obtain a bird straight from the farm, you may have to pluck and draw it yourself. Plucking must always be done first. Working back from the neck to the tail, grasp the feathers close to the skin and pull downwards with a jerk. Large quills which stick in the skin can be pulled out with tweezers.

Hold the plucked bird and turn over a low gas or candle flame to burn off the smallest feathers and the remains of quills.

Jointing Poultry

Many dishes require poultry be divided into portions before cooking. Small chickens can easily be cut once lengthways and once across into 4 portions. Larger chickens can be cut into 6 pieces; duck, geese and turkeys into as many as 8-12 portions.

Cut through the hip joint, remove the legs and divide large legs into thigh and drumstick.

Boning Breast Meat

Domestic poultry is frequently offered for sale in portions, often including the skin and bones. For dishes involving short cooking times, the breast should be boned and skinned; the lean meat is then used as fillets.

First take out the breastbone and centre cartilage, then remove the wishbone.

Stuffing Poultry

The body cavity should never be filled completely with stuffing. The stuffing expands during cooking and the skin might burst. Only stuff poultry two-thirds full. Any leftover stuffing can be cooked separately in the oven in a small lightly greased dish.

Arrange the stuffing loosely in the body cavity using a tablespoon; do not stuff the bird full.

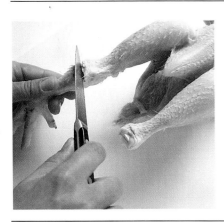

Cut off the head and neck and pull the gullet from the chest cavity. Remove the feet by cutting through the first joint.

Cut open across the body in front of the anus and carefully remove all the innards. Cut open the tail above the anus. Rub residual blood and tissue from the body cavity with 1 tbsp salt, and rinse out with water.

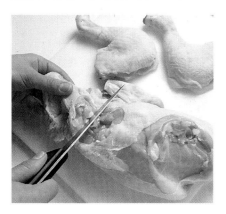

Cut through the shoulder joints with a sharp carving knife and remove the wings. If the bird is large, halve the wings.

Halve the torso lengthways, separate the breast from the ribs, remove the breastbone and halve the breast. Use the back and the smaller pieces in soups and sauces.

Cut through the centre of the breast lengthways, removing any remaining cartilage.

Using a sharp knife, remove the skin from the fillet and pull away with your hand.

Sew both edges of the opening together, using a trussing needle or thick darning needle and trussing thread to make large cross stitches.

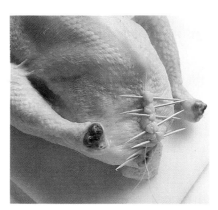

Alternatively, pin the edges of the opening together with wooden cocktail sticks and wind trussing thread around the sticks.

Cooking Poultry

Trussing Poultry

Birds that are to be cooked whole should always be trussed, that is, tied up, before cooking. Trussing thread, a trussing needle or a very long, strong darning needle are required.

Rotate the wing joints, lay and bird on its back and, using the needle, pass the trussing thread from one wing to the other, also securing the skin around the neck. Alternatively, tie the wings together with trussing thread.

Larding Poultry

Before trussing young birds, they should be larded, that is, covered or wrapped in slices of bacon. It is best to use fatty, unsmoked bacon for this.

Both the breasts and thighs of larger birds are larded and then tied together. The bird can then be trussed.

Cooking Poultry on a Spit

The bird should not be too big for the spit; it must not touch the element or block the rotation of the spit. When it is cooked on a barbecue or charcoal spit, the poultry may appear cooked simply because it has a crisp, brown skin, while the inside of the bird is still raw. To avoid this, make sure that the rotating spit is not placed too close to the coals.

All birds that are to be cooked on a spit must be carefully trussed so that no projecting parts can come too close to the heat and burn. If necessary, tie up the bird like a rolled roast.

Poaching Poultry

The bird is cooked just below boiling point in lightly salted water. The heat must be kept as low as possible so that the surface of the liquid is barely bubbling. The fine stock which is produced may be served as an hors d'oeuvre. The main course is the poultry and tender but still crisp vegetables.

Bring the trussed chicken to the boil in lightly salted water, together with an onion studded with cloves, bay leaves and any other vegetables. Skim several times during the first 30 minutes of cooking.

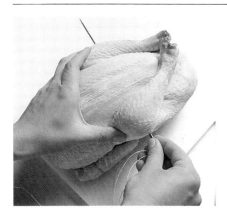

Now pass the needle through both thighs, pull the thread through and tie off.

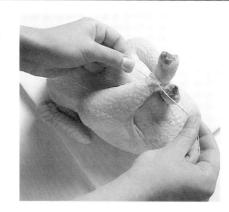

The ends of the legs can also be tied together across the belly using trussing thread.

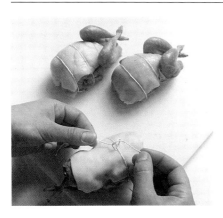

If possible, cover both sides of smaller birds with sufficiently large, thin bacon slices. The bacon slices must be secured using trussing thread.

For special occasions, cut the bacon into strips about 2cm/³/₄ inch wide, weave them together and wrap the bird in them.

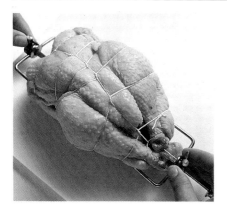

Place the bird lengthways on the spit and attach both ends securely using the adjustable, locking clamps.

If no clamps are fitted to the spit, the bird must either be placed in a trussing basket or fastened to the spit with wire, so that the spit cannot rotate without the bird.

When no more scum forms, adjust the heat so that the stock is just simmering very gently. Poach for about 1¹/₂ hours.

Trim, wash and tie together 2 carrots and 2 white pieces of leek. Poach them with the chicken for the last 30 minutes of the cooking time. Arrange the sliced chicken with the vegetables on a serving plate.

Cooking Poultry

Roasting in Cooking Foil or Roasting Bags

Roasting in foil or a bag is recommended for birds weighing up to 2kg/4¹/₂lbs. It prevents the roast from drying out. Flavoursome ingredients, such as wine, stock and herbs, may be added to the roast. The chicken will be crisp and brown – and the oven stays clean!

Place the prepared trussed poultry in the foil or bag, and add all the other ingredients. Following the instructions on the packaging, seal the foil or bag tightly.

Traditional Roasts

Large birds should be roasted in a roasting tin. Large, fatty poultry should be placed on a rack over a roasting tin so that most of the fat can drain out. All poultry should initially be cooked on the belly. Small birds should be turned when just under half the cooking time has elapsed; a large bird should be laid on one side and cooked on its back only during the final third of the roasting time.

Allow lean, small poultry to brown a little in the oven using dry heat. Cover the ends of the drumsticks with aluminium foil so that they do not burn.

Braising Poultry

Braised dishes are easy to prepare and invariably delicious to eat. Their main advantage is that they produce a delicious gravy or sauce which preserves all the flavour in the best possible way. In addition, you can use almost any combination of vegetables, pulses and other ingredients that you choose.

First, brown the jointed poultry all over in a large flameproof casserole over a high heat – with onions, bacon, garlic and herbs, if desired.

Carving Large Birds

To carve a large bird correctly, you will need a sharp, sturdy knife, a two-pronged fork and a pair of poultry shears or kitchen scissors. Use a large carving board or dish as a base, preferably with a groove around the edge so that any meat juices which may run out are collected rather than lost.

First, cut away the drumsticks and the wings with some of the surrounding muscle.

Place the roast directly on the shelf of the oven. Pierce the top of the foil or bag several times with a needle so that moisture can escape during roasting. Slide the shelf into the oven.

Cut away a corner of the foil or bag when the poultry has cooked, and pour the roasting juices into a pan for making gravy, if liked. Unwrap the poultry, but leave it in the foil or bag, turn off the oven and keep the bird warm.

Roast larger birds in a deep roasting tin. After browning, baste frequently with the hot roasting juices and add more liquid if necessary.

Place a fatty goose on a grid over a roasting tin. Pour boiling water into the tin, and baste the goose with it several times during cooking.

Gradually add boiling water, hot chicken stock or wine, until the poultry portions are covered in about 2cm/³/₄ inch of hot liquid.

Add other vegetables or ingredients according to the recipe and, possibly, additional hot liquid. Cover and braise over a medium heat until cooked.

Hold the body with a fork and carve the breast meat diagonally into slices on both sides.

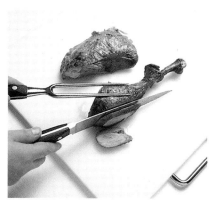

Cut fleshy wings and drumsticks in half and carve thigh meat lengthways into slices if required.

Recommended Cooking Times

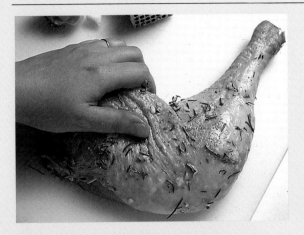

1) Before cooking, spread herbs or herb mixtures evenly over the skin of the poultry after it has been washed and patted dry. Rub in vigorously with your thumb.

2) Pierce the skin of large, fatty birds several times with a darning needle or a wooden cocktail stick to allow fat to run out.

3) Smaller birds and poultry portions should be marinated to improve the flavour. They should also be basted frequently with the roasting juices to prevent the meat from drying out.

	Boiling	Poaching	Braising	Frying pieces
Poussin 300-500g/10oz-1lb 2oz		50 minutes	25-30 minutes	180°C/300°F/gas mark 4 5 minutes 170°C/325°F/gas mark 3 25 minutes (whole)
Corn-fed chicken 600-900g/1¼lbs-2lbs		1½ hours	35-40 minutes	180°C/350°F/gas mark 4 6 minutes 170°C/325°F/gas mark 3 25 minutes (half)
Medium chicken 1-1.4kg/2¼-3lbs		1½ hours	35/45 minutes	180°C/350°F/gas mark 4 8 minutes 170°C/325°F/gas mark 3 30 minutes (half)
Large chicken 1.3-1.6kg/2¾lbs-3lb 10oz	1-1¾ hours	1½-2 hours	45 minutes	180°C/350°F/gas mark 4 10 minutes
Capon 1.5-2kg/3lbs 6oz-4½lbs		3 hours	1 hour	
Boiling fowl 1.7-2kg/3½lbs-4½lbs	2½ hours			
Guinea fowl 800g-1.2kg/1½lbs-2½lbs	1 hour	1½ hours	35-45 minutes	180°C/350°F/gas mark 4 6 minutes
Pigeon 300-400g/10-14oz	1 hour		30-50 minutes	170°C/325°F/gas mark 3 25 minutes (whole)
Duckling 1.6-1.8kg/3½-4lbs			50-70 minutes	
Duck 2-2.5kg/4½lbs-5lbs 6oz			60-80 minutes	
Young fatted goose 4kg/9lbs			1¼-1½ hours	
Goose 5-6kg/11½lbs-13½lbs			1½-2 hours	
Young turkey 2-3kg/4½lbs-6¾lbs				
Turkey 5kg/11¼lbs				
Pheasant 1kg/2¼lbs	1 hour		40-60 minutes	
Partridge 100-400g/4-14oz	1 hour		20-50 minutes	
Quail 100-200g/4-7oz		30-40 minutes	25-40 minutes	
Wild duck 1-2kg/2¼lbs-4¼lbs	2 hours		1-1½ hours	

Tables of cooking times are given purely as a guide. Weight, size, age and quality determine the cooking time of poultry. Cooking at too high a temperature and for too long is more likely to cause harm than good. The way in which individual ovens operate plays a considerable role in successful roasting. You simply have to try your oven out. Depending on the type of oven, it may be a good idea to start roasting at a high temperature and then to continue cooking at lower temperatures.

Roasting	Electric oven	Fan-assisted oven	Gas oven	
stuffed	220°C/425°F 20 minutes 30 minutes	190°C/375°F 20 minutes 30 minutes	Mark 6-7 20 minutes 30 minutes	Poussin 300-500g/10oz-1lb 2oz
stuffed	220°C/425°F 35-40 minutes 45-55 minutes	190°C/375°F 35-40 minutes 45-55 minutes	Mark 6-7 35-40 minutes 45-55 minutes	Corn-fed chicken 600-900g/1¼lbs-2lbs
stuffed	220°C/425°F 40-50 minutes 50-60 minutes	190°C/375°F 40-50 minutes 50-60 minutes	Mark 6-7 40-50 minutes 50-60 minutes	Medium chicken 1-1.4kg/2¼-3lbs
stuffed	200°C/400°F 1 hour 1¼-1½ hours	170°C/325°F 1 hour 1¼-1½ hours	Mark 5-6 1 hour 1¼ hours-1½ hours	Large chicken 1.3-1.6kg/2¾lbs-3lbs 10oz
stuffed	200°C/400°F 1-1¼ hours 1¼-1½ hours	170°C/325°F 1 hour 1¼-1½ hours	Mark 5-6 1-1¼ hours 1¼ hours-1½ hours	Capon 1.5-2kg/3lbs 6oz-4½lbs
				Boiling fowl 1.7-2kg/3½lbs-4½lbs
stuffed	220°C/425°F 30-45 minutes 45-60 minutes	170°C/325°F 30-45 minutes 45-60 minutes	Mark 6-7 30-45 minutes 45-60 minutes	Guinea fowl 800g-1.2kg/1½lbs-2½lbs
stuffed	200°C/400°F 20-30 minutes 30-45 minutes	170°C/325°F 20-30 minutes 30-45 minutes	Mark 6-7 20-30 minutes 30-45 minutes	Pigeon 300-400g/10-14 oz
stuffed	200°C/400°F 1-1½ hours 1¼-1½ hours	170°C/325°F 1-1½ hours 1¼-1½ hours	Mark 5-6 1-1½ hours 1¼-1½ hours	Duckling 1.6-1.8kg/3½lbs-4lbs
stuffed	180°C/350°F 2 hours 2½ hours	160°C/325°F 2 hours 2½ hours	Mark 4 2 hours 2½ hours	Duck 2-2.5kg/4½lbs-5lbs 6oz
stuffed	180°C/350°F 2½ hours 3 hours	160°C/325°F 2½ hours 3 hours	Mark 4 2½ hours 3 hours	Young fatted goose 4kg/9lbs
stuffed	180°C/350°F 3½ hours 4 hours	150°C/300°F 3½ hours 4 hours	Mark 4 3½ hours 4 hours	Fatted goose 5-6kg/11¼lbs-13½lbs
stuffed	180°C/350°F 2½ hours 3 hours	160°C/325°F 2½ hours 3 hours	Mark 4 2½ hours 3 hours	Young turkey 2-3kg/4½lbs-6¾lbs
stuffed	180°C/350°F 3 hours 3½ hours	150°C/300°F 3 hours 3½ hours	Mark 4 3 hours 3½ hours	Turkey 5kg/1¼lbs
stuffed	220°C/425°F 30-40 minutes 45-60 minutes	190°C/375°F 30-40 minutes 45-60 minutes	Mark 6-7 30-40 minutes 45-60 minutes	Pheasant 1kg/2¾lbs
stuffed	220°C/425°F 35-40 minutes 45-50 minutes	190°C/375°F 35-40 minutes 45-50 minutes	Mark 6-7 35-40 minutes 45-50 minutes	Partridge 100-400g/4-14 oz
stuffed	220°C/425°F 20 minutes 30 minutes	190°C/375°F 20 minutes 30 minutes	Mark 6-7 20 minutes 30 minutes	Quail 100-200g/4-7oz
stuffed	180°C/350°F 1½ hours 1¾-2 hours	170°C/325°F 1½ hours 1¾-2 hours	Mark 4 1½ hours 1¾-2 hours	Wild duck 1-2kg/2¼lbs-4½lbs

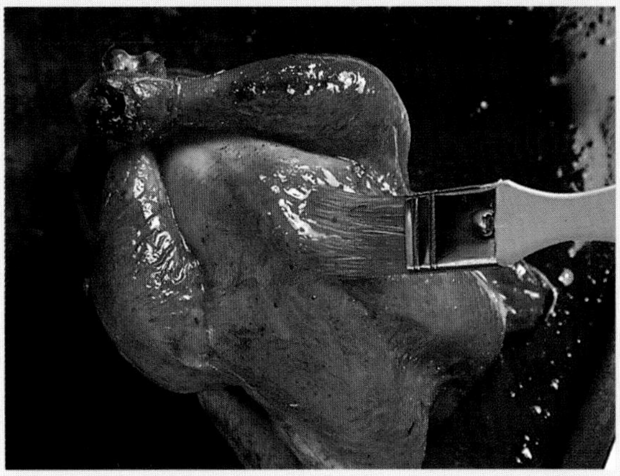

4) Depending on the size of the bird and the time it takes to roast, brush the skin several times with marinade, salted water, honey and water, beer or wine 15-30 minutes before the end of the roasting time, so that it turns lovely and crisp.

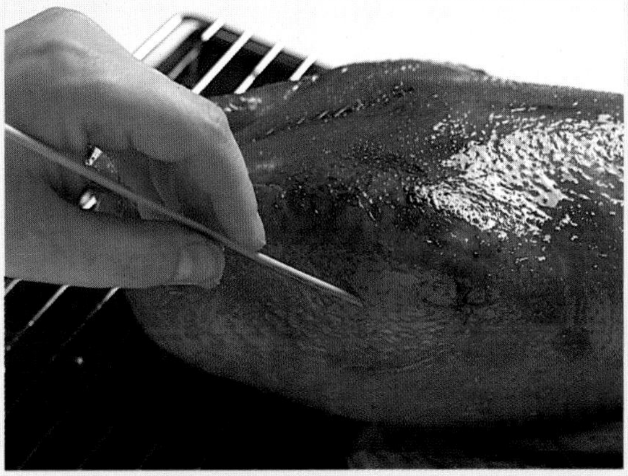

5) When two-thirds of the recommended cooking time has elapsed, test to see if the bird is cooked to avoid over-cooking. Pierce the thigh. If the meat juices are colourless with no trace of pink, then it is ready.

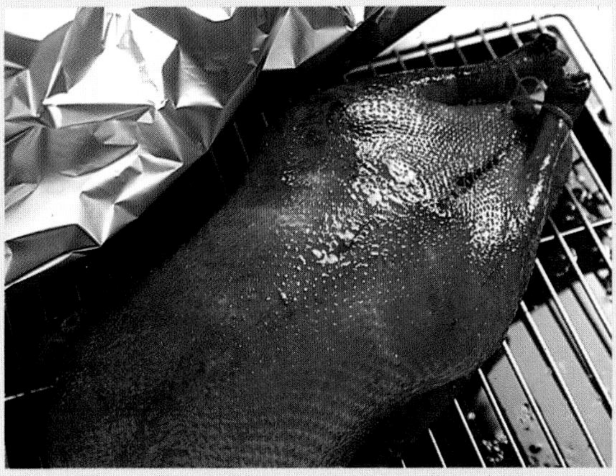

6) Turn the oven off and leave the cooked poultry to rest for about 10 minutes before carving. Take the roast out of the juices and wrap loosely in aluminium foil.

Delicious Soups and Hearty Stews

Starters for dinner parties,
and light main meals

Cream of Chicken Soup

Suitable as an hors d'oeuvre on special occasions

1 x 1kg/2¼lbs chicken
2l/2½ pints water
Salt
3 leeks
1 carrot • 1 celery stalk
1 onion
2 cloves
½ bay leaf
1 tbsp finely chopped fresh parsley
2 white peppercorns
50g/2oz butter
3 tbsps flour
2 egg yolks
125ml/4fl oz double cream

Preparation time: 40 minutes
Cooking time: 2 hours
Nutritional value:
Analysis per serving, approx:
• 3900kJ/930kcal
• 54g protein
• 70g fat
• 23g carbohydrate

Rinse the chicken and pat dry. Place in a saucepan, add the water and a pinch of salt, and bring to the boil. Lower the heat and simmer for 1½ hours. Skim repeatedly during the first 30 minutes. The stock should reduce by half during cooking time. • Trim, halve and wash the leeks. Peel and slice the carrot. Wash and slice the celery. Stud the onion with the cloves. • Add the leeks, carrot, celery, onion, cloves, bay leaf, parsley and peppercorns. Cover, and cook for a further 30 minutes. • Remove the chicken from the soup. Cut off the breast meat and remove and discard the skin. Slice the breast meat. • Rub the stock through a sieve, reserving the leek, and set aside to cool. Skim off the fat and discard. Chop the leek. • Melt the butter in a large pan, stir in the flour and cook, stirring constantly, for 1-2 minutes. Gradually stir in 1l/1¾ pints of the chicken stock. Bring to the boil, stirring constantly. Lower the heat and simmer for 10 minutes. • Add the chicken breast and the leek to the soup. • Beat the egg yolks with the cream. Stir into the soup and heat, stirring constantly, until thickened.

Spicy and Mild Chicken Soups

Soups to suit all tastes

Mild Chicken Soup
Illustrated left

1 x 1kg/2¹/₄lbs chicken
1.5l/2¹/₂ pints water
1 bunch flat-leafed parsley
Salt
500g/1lb 2oz cooking apples
1 tsp clear honey
1 tbsp oatmeal
125ml/4fl oz soured cream
1 egg yolk

Preparation time: 30 minutes
Cooking time: 1¹/₂ hours
Nutritional value:
Analysis per serving, approx:
• 2000kJ/480kcal
• 54g protein • 22g fat
• 21g carbohydrate

Wash the chicken, pat dry and divide into 8 pieces. Place in a saucepan, add the water and bring to the boil. Lower the heat and simmer for 30 minutes, skimming frequently. • Wash the parsley and shake dry. Chop the leaves and set aside. Reserve the stalks. • Add the parsley stalks to the soup, and season to taste with salt. Cook for a further 50 minutes. • Peel, quarter, core and slice the apples. Place in pan, add the honey and 4 tbsps of water. Cook over a low heat until just soft. • Remove the parsley stalks and the chicken pieces from the soup. Skin, bone and dice the chicken. • Dry-fry the oatmeal until light brown. Stir the oatmeal into the soured cream. Stir the soured cream mixture into the soup, and simmer for a further 5 minutes. • Add the chicken and the apple slices, and warm through. Remove the soup from the heat. • Beat the egg yolk with 2 tbsps of the hot soup. Stir into the soup and cook, stirring constantly, until thickened. Serve sprinkled with the chopped parsley.

Spicy Chicken Soup
Illustrated right

1 x 500g/1lb 2oz stock pack or frozen chicken giblets
1.5l/2¹/₂ pints water
1 bouquet garni
Salt
200g/7oz skinned chicken fillets
100g/4oz mushrooms
1 onion
15g/¹/₂oz butter
1 tbsp curry powder
Pinch cayenne
2 tbsps snipped chives

Defrosting time: 4 hours
Preparation time: 20 minutes
Cooking time: 1 hour
Nutritional value:
Analysis per serving, approx:
• 1100kJ/260kcal
• 38g protein
• 13g fat
• 2g carbohydrate

Defrost the stock pack or chicken giblets. Discard the liquid that is produced. • Rinse the giblets, and place in a pan. Add the water, and bring to the boil. Lower the heat and simmer for 30 minutes, skimming several times. • Add the bouquet garni, and season to taste with salt. Cook for a further 30 minutes. • Slice the chicken breasts into matchstick strips. Rinse, pat dry and slice the mushrooms. • Peel and finely chop the onion. • Melt the butter in a pan, and fry the onion until transparent. Add the chicken strips, and fry until they turn white. Add the mushrooms, and fry for 1 minute. Mix together the curry powder and cayenne. • Rub the chicken stock through a sieve and discard the giblets and bouquet garni. Stir in the curry and cayenne mixture. Pour the stock over the meat and keep warm. • Serve the soup sprinkled with the chives.

Velvety Cream of Chicken Soup

One with green asparagus, the other with a touch of apple and banana

Cream of Chicken and Asparagus

Illustrated right

750g/1¹/₂lbs chicken pieces
1.75l/3 pints water
3 tbsps finely chopped mixed fresh herbs • 1 bay leaf
5 white peppercorns • Sea salt
400g/14oz green asparagus
150g/5oz shelled green peas
50g/2oz wholemeal flour
125ml/4fl oz double cream
2 egg yolks • Juice of ¹/₂ lemon
2 tbsps chopped fresh chervil

Preparation time: 30 minutes

Cooking time: 1¹/₂ hours

Nutritional value:
Analysis per serving, approx:
• 2050kJ/490kcal • 43g protein
• 49g fat • 17g carbohydrate

Rinse the chicken pieces and place in a pan. Add the water, mixed herbs, bay leaf and peppercorns, and bring to the boil. Season to taste with salt. Simmer for 1 hour 20 minutes. • Wash the asparagus. Carefully peel the lower parts. Cut the asparagus tips into 5cm/2-inch pieces and set aside. • Chop the asparagus spears. Add to the stock, and cook for a further 10 minutes. • Remove the chicken pieces and set aside. Rub the stock through a sieve, reserving the asparagus spears. Measure 1l/1³/₄ pints of the stock. Reserve the remaining stock and set aside to cool. • Put the measured stock in a saucepan, and bring back to the boil. Add the asparagus pieces, the asparagus tips and the peas, and cook for 5 minutes. • Skin the chicken pieces and cut the meat from the bones. Dice the meat, and add to the soup. • Stir the flour into 250ml/9fl oz of reserved cold chicken stock. Stir it into the soup. Cook, stirring constantly, for 5 minutes. Remove from the heat. • Beat together the cream and egg yolks, and stir into the soup. Stir in the lemon juice, season and sprinkle with the chopped chervil.

Cream of Chicken and Bananas

Illustrated left

500g/1lb 2oz frozen stock pack or chicken giblets
1.2l/2¹/₄ pints water
1 bouquet garni
Salt and freshly ground white pepper • 1 onion
50g/2oz butter • 2 tbsps flour
1 cooking apple • 2 bananas
4 tbsps double cream
2 tsps lemon juice
1 tbsp toasted flaked almonds

Defrosting time: 4 hours

Preparation time: 40 minutes

Cooking time: 1 hour

Nutritional value:
Analysis per serving, approx:
• 1600kJ/380kcal • 28g protein
• 22g fat • 21g carbohydrate

Defrost the stock pack or chicken giblets. Rinse, and place in a pan. Add the water, and bring to the boil. Lower the heat, and simmer for 30 minutes, skimming several times. • Add the bouquet garni and season to taste with salt. Cook for a further 30 minutes. • Rub the stock through a sieve, reserving the meat. Discard the bouquet garni. Separate the meat from the bones and dice. Chop the chicken liver, and return to the pan with the stock. • Peel and finely chop the onion. Melt the butter, and fry the onion until transparent. Sprinkle over the flour, and fry gently until lightly coloured. Stir the onion and flour mixture into the stock. Bring to the boil, stirring constantly. Cook for a further 10 minutes. • Peel and finely grate the apple. Peel the bananas, mash 1 and finely slice the other. Stir the mashed banana, cream, grated apple and lemon juice into the soup. • Season to taste with pepper. Serve the soup sprinkled with the sliced banana and the toasted almonds.

Duck Soup with a Pastry Lid

Ovenproof soup bowls are needed for this recipe

250g/8oz duck breast
1 tsp sunflower oil
Salt and freshly ground white pepper • 2 spring onions
250g/8oz courgettes
100g/4oz mushrooms
750ml/1¼ pints chicken stock
150g/5oz veal sausage meat
2 tbsps finely chopped fresh chervil • 4 tbsps double cream
4 sheets frozen rough puff pastry, thawed • 1 egg yolk

Preparation time: 40 minutes
Cooking time: 15 minutes
Nutritional value:
Analysis per serving, approx:
• 2300kJ/550kcal • 25g protein
• 36g fat • 32g carbohydrate

Wash and dry the duck breast. Heat the oil, and fry the duck, skin side down, until browned. Turn and fry for a further 3 minutes or until cooked. Remove from the pan and drain on kitchen paper. Season to taste with salt and pepper. • Trim, wash and slice the spring onions. Wash, pat dry and dice the courgettes. Wash, pat dry and slice the mushrooms. • Place the chicken stock in a pan and bring to the boil. • Mix together the sausage meat, chervil and 2 tbsps of cream, and season to taste with pepper. Using a damp teaspoon, shape dumplings from the mixture. Add the dumplings to the stock, and simmer for 10 minutes. • Slice the duck breast into matchstick strips and divide between two large soup bowls. Divide the spring onions, courgettes and mushrooms between the bowls. • Roll out the dough on a lightly floured surface into circles 2cm/³/₄ inch larger than the diameter of the bowls. Beat the egg yolk with the remaining cream. • Fill the bowls with the hot soup and the dumplings. Lay the dough circles over the tops of the bowls, and seal the edges. Brush the surface of the dough with the egg yolk and cream mixture. • Bake in a preheated oven at 220°C/425°F/gas mark 7 for about 15 minutes, or until the pastry has risen and is golden.

Poultry and Game Soups from Hungary and Poland

Tasty, hearty ways of cooking chicken and pheasant

Hungarian Chicken Soup
Illustrated left

750g/1lb 8oz chicken pieces
100g/4oz carrots • 2 celery stalks
100g/4oz cauliflower
1 garlic clove
1 beefsteak tomato • 1 onion
1 sprig parsley
6 black peppercorns • Salt
50g/2oz French beans
50g/2oz shelled peas
50g/2oz vermicelli

Preparation time: 30 minutes
Cooking time: 1¼ hours
Nutritional value:
Analysis per serving, approx:
• 2500kJ/600kcal • 41g protein
• 39g fat • 23g carbohydrate

Wash the chicken pieces and pat dry. Peel the carrots and cut half of them into matchstick strips, leaving the others whole.

Cut 1 celery stalk into matchstick strips. Cut the other in half. • Wash the cauliflower and divide into florets. • Peel the garlic. Quarter the tomato. Peel and roughly chop the onion. • Place the chicken pieces in a pan, cover with cold water and bring to the boil. • Add the whole carrots and halved celery stalk, garlic, tomato, onion, parsley and peppercorns, and season to taste with salt. Bring to the boil again, lower the heat and simmer for 1 hour. Skim frequently during this time. • Slice the beans. Add the carrot and celery strips, cauliflower florets, beans and peas to a pan of lightly salted boiling water, cover and cook for 10 minutes. Drain. • Cook the vermicelli in 500ml/16 fl oz boiling water for 3 minutes and drain. • Skin the chicken and cut the meat from the bones. Dice the chicken meat and place in a tureen. Add the vermicelli, carrot strips, celery strips, cauliflower, peas and beans. • Strain over the stock, and discard the stock vegetables. Serve the soup immediately.

Polish Pheasant Soup
Illustrated right

1 x 1kg/2¼lbs pheasant
1.5l/2½ pints water
6 black peppercorns
1 bay leaf • Salt
2 carrots • 1 leek
3 tbsps sunflower oil
1 tbsp wholemeal flour
125ml/4fl oz crème fraîche
2 tbsps finely chopped fresh parsley

Preparation time: 45 minutes
Cooking time: 1½ hours
Nutritional value:
Analysis per serving, approx:
• 2300kJ/550kcal • 55g protein
• 35g fat
• 10g carbohydrate

Wash the pheasant. Place in a pan, add the water, peppercorns and bay leaf, and season with salt to taste. Bring to the boil and cook over a high heat for 1 hour. • Peel and slice the carrots. Trim and wash the leek and slice into thin rings. • Remove the cooked pheasant from the stock and set aside. Remove and discard the bay leaf. Rub the stock through a sieve. • Heat the oil in a pan, and fry the carrots and leek, stirring constantly, until lightly coloured. Add the flour and cook, stirring constantly, for 3 minutes or until golden. Gradually stir in the vegetable stock. Bring to the boil, lower the heat and simmer for 10 minutes. • Skin the pheasant and cut the meat from the bones. Dice the meat. • Add to the soup and heat through. Remove from the heat, and stir in the crème fraîche. • Serve the soup sprinkled with the parsley.

Speciality Soups

Unusual but delicious – definitely worth a try

'Sapporo' Chicken Soup

Illustrated left

500g/1lb 2oz chicken breast fillets
50g/2oz white radish
50g/2oz carrot
200g/7oz potatoes
50g/2oz leek, white part only
200g/7oz French beans
2 tbsps sunflower oil
1l/1³⁄₄ pints strong chicken stock
5 tbsps soya sauce
2 tsps honey
1 tsp green peppercorns
Salt
100g/4oz cooked peeled prawns

Preparation time: 45 minutes
Cooking time: 15 minutes
Nutritional value:
Analysis per serving, approx:
• 1100kJ/260kcal
• 36g protein • 7g fat
• 16g carbohydrate

Wash, pat dry and dice the chicken. • Peel the radish, carrot and potatoes and cut into matchstick strips. Trim, halve and wash the leek. Pat dry and cut into matchstick strips. • Wash the beans and pat dry. • Heat the oil, and fry the chicken until golden brown. Add the radish, carrot, potato, leek and beans, and stir-fry for 5 minutes. • Heat the chicken stock. Add to the pan, cover and simmer for 15 minutes. Add the soya sauce, honey and green peppercorns. Season to taste with salt. Stir in the prawns, and heat through.

Guinea Fowl and Courgette Soup

Illustrated right

1 x 800g/1lb 8oz guinea fowl
1.5l/2¹⁄₂ pints water
Salt
1 onion
1 clove
¹⁄₂ bay leaf
500g/1lb 2oz courgettes
1 bunch of watercress or 1 punnet mustard and cress

Preparation time: 30 minutes
Cooking time: 1 hour
Nutritional value:
Analysis per serving, approx:
• 1300kJ/310kcal
• 44g protein
• 14g fat
• 9g carbohydrate

Wash the guinea fowl, place in a saucepan, add the water and season to taste with salt. Bring to the boil, lower the heat and simmer for 30 minutes. Skim frequently during this time. • Peel the onion and stud with the clove. • Add the onion, clove and bay leaf to the pan, and cook for a further 20 minutes. The liquid should reduce by at least half during this time. • Trim, wash, pat dry and dice the courgettes. Wash the watercress and shake dry, if using. Remove and discard the large stalks. Roughly chop the leaves. Cut, wash and shake dry the mustard and cress, if using. • Add the diced courgette to the pan, cover and cook for a further 10 minutes. • Remove the bay leaf and the onion and discard. Continue to cook the soup until the guinea fowl is tender. • Remove the guinea fowl from the soup. Skin and cut the meat from the bones. Dice the meat and add to the soup. • Serve sprinkled with the watercress or mustard and cress.

Mulligatawny

This spicy and satisfying soup originated in India

100g/4oz long-grain rice

1.2l/2 pints chicken stock

50g/2oz raisins

500g/1lb 2oz skinned chicken breast fillets

100g/4oz carrots

100g/4oz leek, white part only

2 tbsps vegetable oil

1 cooking apple

1 tbsp curry powder

$^1/_4$ tsp cayenne

4 tbsps grated coconut

Preparation time: 35 minutes
Nutritional value:
Analysis per serving, approx:
• 1900kJ/450kcal
• 33g protein
• 19g fat
• 38g carbohydrate

Rinse the rice under cold running water. • Bring the chicken stock to the boil. Add the rice, and simmer for 20 minutes. • Soak the raisins in hot water while the rice is cooking, changing the water several times. • Wash the chicken fillets, pat dry and dice. Peel the carrots and cut into short matchstick strips. Trim and wash the leek and cut into rings. • Heat the oil, and stir-fry the chicken until tender. Remove the chicken from the pan, drain on kitchen paper and set aside. Fry the carrots and leek in the same pan for 5 minutes. Remove from the pan and drain on kitchen paper. Add the diced chicken, carrots and leek to the soup. • Drain the raisins. Peel and grate the apple. Stir the raisins and the apple into the soup. • Stir in the curry powder and cayenne. Serve immediately, sprinkled with the grated coconut.

Vegetable Stews with Chicken

Vegetables and poultry complement each other perfectly and make light dishes that are easy to digest

Chicken and Rice Stew
Illustrated left

1 x 1kg/2¹/₄lbs chicken
1.5l/2¹/₂ pints water
500g/1lb 2oz peas
200g/7oz carrots
1 sprig tarragon
1 sprig thyme
1 sprig parsley
1 sprig celery leaves
100g/4oz leek, white part only
2 shallots • Salt
200g/7oz long-grain rice
1/4 tsp cayenne
2 tbsps finely chopped fresh parsley

Preparation time: 30 minutes
Cooking time: 1 hour 20 minutes
Nutritional value:
Analysis per serving, approx:
• 2680kJ/640kcal • 65g protein
• 18g fat • 63g carbohydrate

Rinse the chicken and place in a pan. Add the water and bring to the boil. Lower the heat and simmer for 30 minutes. Skim frequently during this time. • Meanwhile, shell the peas. Peel and dice the carrots. Wash the tarragon, thyme, parsley and celery sprigs, and tie them together. Trim and wash the leeks, and cut into rings. Peel and quarter the shallots. • Add the bunch of herbs, leeks and shallots to the pan, and season to taste with salt. Cover and cook for a further 30 minutes. • Wash the rice under cold running water. • Remove the chicken from the stock and set aside. Remove the herbs and discard. Add the peas, carrots and rice to the stock, cover and cook over a low heat for 20 minutes. • Skin the chicken and cut the meat from the bones. Dice the meat and add to the rice. Season with the cayenne and serve sprinkled with the chopped parsley.

Chicken and Vegetable Stew
Illustrated right

1 x 1kg/2¹/₄lbs chicken
1 onion
1 carrot
2 leeks, white parts only
40g/1¹/₂oz butter
2 tsps mild paprika
Salt and freshly ground white pepper
250ml/8fl oz apple juice
400g/14oz tomatoes
100g/4oz mushrooms
2 tbsps snipped chives

Preparation time: 1¹/₄ hours
Nutritional value:
Analysis per serving, approx:
• 2200kJ/520kcal
• 55g protein
• 30g fat
• 15g carbohydrate

Wash the chicken and divide into 8 pieces. • Peel and chop the onion. Peel and dice the carrot. Trim and wash the leeks and slice into rings. • Heat 25g/1oz of the butter in a large flameproof casserole. Fry the chicken pieces, turning occasionally, for 10 minutes until golden and crisp. Remove the chicken from the casserole and set aside. • Fry the onion and carrot in the casserole until lightly coloured. Add the remaining butter, and fry the leeks until lightly coloured. Place the chicken pieces on top of the vegetables. Sprinkle over the paprika, and season to taste with salt and pepper. Pour over the apple juice and bring to the boil. Lower the heat, cover and simmer for 25 minutes. • Skin the tomatoes and cut into 8. Wipe and thinly slice the mushrooms. Add the tomatoes and mushrooms to the casserole, and cook for a further 10 minutes. • Serve the stew sprinkled with the chives.

Chicken and Swede Stew

The flavours of chicken and swede complement each other in this tasty stew

1 x 1.2kg/2½lbs chicken
1.5l/2½ pints water
1 bouquet garni
5 white peppercorns
Sea salt and freshly ground black pepper
1kg/2¼lbs swedes or kohlrabi
250g/8oz shallots
2 tbsps finely chopped fresh parsley

Preparation time: 45 minutes
Cooking time: 1 hour 25 minutes
Nutritional value:
Analysis per serving, approx:
• 2300kJ/550kcal
• 66g protein
• 21g fat
• 30g carbohydrate

Wash the chicken, place in a pan, and add the water, the bouquet garni and the peppercorns. Season to taste with salt and bring to the boil. Lower the heat and simmer for 1 hour. Skim frequently during the first 30 minutes. • Peel and dice the swedes or kohlrabi. Peel and quarter the shallots. • Remove the chicken from the stock and set aside. Remove the bouquet garni and discard. Cook the swedes and shallots in the chicken stock for 25 minutes. • Skin the chicken and cut the meat from the bones. Dice the meat, and add to the pan. Stir in the parsley, and season to taste with salt and pepper. • Serve with crusty farmhouse bread.

Chicken Stew with Mixed Vegetables

A filling winter dish

To serve 6:
500g/1lb 2oz carrots
400g/14oz celery
400g/14oz leeks
1 onion • 2 garlic cloves
1 thyme sprig • 1 bay leaf
1 clove • 1.5l/2½ pints water
1 tsp white peppercorns
Sea salt and freshly ground white pepper
1 x 1.8kg/4lbs chicken
2 heads kohlrabi
400g/14oz courgettes

Preparation time: 40 minutes
Cooking time: 2 hours 10 minutes
Nutritional value:
Analysis per serving, approx:
• 3800kJ/900kcal • 62g protein
• 62g fat • 26g carbohydrate

Peel the carrots and finely dice 2 of them. Wash, trim and finely dice the celery. Trim and wash the leeks and finely dice 1. Peel and dice the onion and the garlic cloves. Place the diced carrots, celery, diced leek, garlic, thyme, bay leaf, clove, water and peppercorns in a pan, and season to taste with salt. • Wash the chicken, and add to the pan. Bring to the boil, lower the heat and simmer for 2 hours. Skim frequently during the first 30 minutes. • Slice the remaining leek into rings. Peel the kohlrabi. Trim and wash the courgettes. Slice the kohlrabi, courgettes and the remaining carrots into matchstick strips. • Remove the chicken from the stock. Remove and discard the thyme, bay leaf and clove. Rub the stock through a sieve. Return to the saucepan with the matchstick vegetables. Bring to the boil, lower the heat and simmer for about 10 minutes. • Skin the chicken and cut the meat from the bones. Dice the meat. Add the meat to the pan, heat through and season to taste with salt and pepper.

Traditional Poultry Dishes

These specialities prove that tasty can also mean economical

Sweet and Sour Goose Pieces
Illustrated left

250g/8oz mixed dried fruit salad
1kg/2¼lbs goose pieces
750ml/1¼ pints water
1 onion • 2 cloves
1 bay leaf • 1 bouquet garni
Salt and freshly ground black pepper
50g/2oz butter • 5 tbsps flour
2 tbsps vinegar • 1 tbsp sugar

Soaking time: 12 hours
Preparation time: 25 minutes
Cooking time: 1½ hours
Nutritional value:
Analysis per serving, approx:
• 3100kJ/740kcal • 23g protein
• 48g fat • 57g carbohydrate

Place the dried fruit in a bowl, cover with cold water and leave to soak for 12 hours. • Wash the goose pieces. Place the goose pieces and water in a pan, bring to the boil and skim. • Peel the onion and stud with the cloves. Add the onion, cloves, bay leaf and the bouquet garni to the pan, and season to taste with salt. Cover and cook over a low heat for 30 minutes. Add the dried fruit and its soaking liquid, cover, and cook for a further 30 minutes. The stock should reduce by at least one third during the cooking time. • Remove the goose pieces and the dried fruit from the stock and set aside. Remove the bouquet garni and discard. Rub the stock through a sieve and reserve 500ml/16fl oz. • Melt the butter, and stir in the flour. Cook, stirring constantly, for 3 minutes or until golden. Gradually stir in the reserved stock and simmer for 10 minutes, stirring occasionally. • Stir in the vinegar and sugar, and season to taste with salt and pepper. • Add the dried fruit and the goose pieces, and heat through. • Dumplings make an excellent accompaniment.

Pörkölt Chicken
Illustrated right

To serve 6:

1 x 1.5kg/3lbs 6oz chicken, with giblets • 2l/3½ pints water
1 bouquet garni
Salt and freshly ground white pepper
100g/4oz rindless streaky bacon
4 onions • 2 green peppers
2 beefsteak tomatoes
1 tbsp sunflower oil
2 tbsps paprika

Preparation time: 1 hour
Cooking time: 2 hours
Nutritional value:
Analysis per serving, approx:
• 3400kJ/810kcal • 50g protein
• 63g fat • 9g carbohydrate

Wash the chicken and the giblets. Set aside the liver, and place the chicken and the remaining giblets in a pan. Add the water and the bouquet garni, and season. Bring to the boil, skim, lower the heat and simmer for 1½ hours. • Dice the bacon. Peel and chop the onions. Halve, core, seed and wash the peppers. Cut into matchstick strips. Skin the tomatoes and cut into wedges. • Remove the chicken and the giblets from the stock. Divide the chicken into 12 pieces and dice the giblets. Remove the bouquet garni and discard. Rub the stock through a sieve and reserve 500ml/16fl oz. • Heat the oil, and fry the bacon until the fat begins to run. Add the chicken pieces, and fry until golden on all sides. Add the onions and peppers, and fry until the onions are lightly coloured. Stir in the paprika. • Place the reserved stock in a pan. Add the chicken pieces, onions, peppers and giblets, and cook for 10 minutes. • Chop the reserved chicken liver. Add the liver and tomatoes to the pan, and simmer for a further 10 minutes. Season to taste.

Vegetable Stews with Goose

Good for using up roast goose left-overs, as well as for cooking a small fresh goose

Stewed Goose in Savoy Cabbage
Illustrated left

To serve 8:

20g/³/₄oz rindless bacon
3 carrots • 2 onions
1kg/2¹/₄lbs savoy cabbage
1 x 3kg/6³/₄lbs goose
15g/¹/₂oz butter
125ml/4fl oz full-bodied red wine
Salt and freshly ground black pepper
1 tbsp tomato purée
125ml/4fl oz chicken stock

Preparation time: 1 hour
Cooking time: 1¹/₂ hours
Nutritional value:
Analysis per serving, approx:
• 4000kJ/940kcal • 44g protein
• 81g fat • 11g carbohydrate

Finely dice the bacon. Peel and thinly slice the carrots. Peel, quarter and thinly slice the onions.

• Quarter the cabbage and discard the stem and tough outer leaves. Wash the cabbage, shake dry and shred coarsely. • Wash the goose and pat dry. Divide the goose into 16 pieces. • Melt the butter in a large flameproof casserole. Add the bacon and the goose pieces, and fry until the goose is crisp and golden. Remove the goose pieces and set aside. • Add the carrots and onions, and fry gently for 10 minutes. Add the cabbage and the wine, season to taste with salt and pepper and cook for a further 1-2 minutes. Return all the goose pieces except the breast. • Mix together the tomato purée and chicken stock. Add the stock mixture to the casserole, cover and cook in a preheated oven at 180°C/350 F°/gas mark 4 for 1 hour. • Add the goose breast, return the casserole to the oven and cook for a further 30 minutes.

Goose and Swede Stew
Illustrated right

1 goose carcass
600g/1¹/₄lbs roast goose meat
175 ml/6fl oz goose gravy
500 ml/16fl oz water
500g/1lb 2oz swedes
250g/8oz potatoes
250g/8oz carrots • 2 onions
50g/2oz lard
1 tbsp flour
Salt and freshly ground white pepper
2 tbsps finely chopped fresh parsley

Preparation time: 40 minutes
Cooking time: 50 minutes
Nutritional value:
Analysis per serving, approx:
• 3300kJ/790kcal
• 28g protein
• 59g fat
• 34g carbohydrate

Cut the goose carcass into pieces using poultry shears. Remove the skin from the goose meat, slice the meat and set aside. Place the carcass, skin, gravy and water in a pan and bring to the boil. Lower the heat, cover and simmer for 30 minutes. • Peel and dice the swedes, potatoes and carrots. • Rub the goose stock through a sieve. • Peel and chop the onions. Melt the lard, and fry the onions until transparent. Stir in the flour and gradually add the goose stock. Add the swedes, cover, and cook for 20 minutes. • Add the potatoes and carrots and season to taste with salt. Cover and cook for a further 20 minutes. Add the goose meat and heat through. • Season to taste with pepper and serve sprinkled with the chopped parsley.

Fruity Cock-a-Leekie

An exotic variation on a traditional Scottish theme

1 x 1kg/2¹/₄bs chicken
1 chicken heart
10 prunes
1 onion
6 tbsps pearl barley
Salt and freshly ground black pepper
800g/1¹/₂lbs leeks
1 chicken liver
2 tbsps finely chopped fresh parsley

Preparation time: 40 minutes
Cooking time: 1¹/₂ hours
Nutritional value:
Analysis per serving, approx:
- 2300kJ/550kcal
- 59g protein
- 18g fat
- 44g carbohydrate

Wash the chicken. Place the chicken, chicken heart and the prunes in a pan, and add enough water just to cover. Bring to the boil and skim. Lower the heat. • Peel and finely chop the onion. Add the onion and pearl barley to the pan, and season to taste with salt and pepper. Cover and poach over a very low heat for 1¹/₄ hours. The surface of the water should be barely rippling. • Trim and wash the leeks and cut into rings. • Add the leeks and the chicken liver to the pan, and cook for a further 15 minutes. • Remove the cooked chicken and giblets from the stock. Skin the chicken and cut the meat from the bones. Thinly slice the meat and giblets. • Return the pan to fairly high heat and boil vigorously until the stock has reduced by one third. • Add the chicken meat and giblets, and heat through. Season to taste with salt and pepper. • Serve sprinkled with the parsley.

Waterzooi

A Flemish soup that can also be made with fish instead of chicken and beef

200g/7oz brisket of beef

6 red peppers • 1.2l/2 pints water

6 peppercorns • Salt

1 x 1.2kg/2½lbs chicken, with giblets • 200g/7oz leeks

100g/4oz celery

200g/7oz carrots • 1 onion

50g/2oz butter • 2 tbsps flour

2 egg yolks

6 tbsps double cream

2 tsps lemon juice

Preparation time: 40 minutes
Cooking time: 1½ hours
Nutritional value:
Analysis per serving, approx:
• 2900kJ/690kcal • 76g protein
• 41g fat • 16g carbohydrate

Rinse the beef. Halve, seed, wash and coarsely chop the peppers. Place the beef, water, peppers and peppercorns in a large pan, and season to taste with salt. Bring to the boil and skim. Lower the heat and simmer for 45 minutes. • Using poultry shears, cut the chicken in half. Rinse the chicken and the giblets. Add to the pan, and cook for a further 45 minutes. • Trim and wash the leeks and the celery. Peel the carrots. Cut the leeks, celery and carrot into large pieces. Peel and halve the onion. Add the leeks, celery, carrots and onion to the pan, and cook for a further 30 minutes. • Remove the beef, chicken, giblets, carrots, leeks and celery from the stock and set aside. (Reserve the beef and the giblets to use in another recipe). Remove the onion and discard. Rub the stock through a sieve. Slice the carrots. Cut the leeks into rings and dice the celery. • Melt the butter, and stir in the flour. Cook, stirring constantly, for 3 minutes or until golden. Gradually stir in the stock and bring to the boil, stirring constantly. Lower the heat and simmer for 1-2 minutes, stirring occasionally. • Skin the chicken and cut the meat from the bones. Slice the chicken meat. Add the chicken, carrots, leeks and celery to the pan, and heat through. • Remove the pan from the heat. Beat together the egg yolks and cream, and stir into the soup. Stir in the lemon juice, and season to taste with salt.

Chicken and Pasta Stew

This dish is both healthy and delicious

1 x 1kg/2¼lbs chicken ,with giblets • 3 red peppers	
1.5l/2½ pints water	
3 peppercorns • ½ bay leaf	
Salt • 1 bouquet garni	
1 onion • 2 garlic cloves	
250g/8oz aubergines	
250g/8oz courgettes	
250g/8oz small tomatoes	
1 tbsp sunflower oil	
2 tsps finely chopped fresh thyme	
100g/4oz pasta bows	

Preparation time: 50 minutes
Cooking time: 1½ hours
Nutritional value:
Analysis per serving, approx:
• 2100kJ/500kcal • 58g protein
• 20g fat • 59g carbohydrate

Rinse the chicken and the giblets. Halve, seed, wash and coarsely chop the peppers. Place the chicken, giblets, water, peppers, peppercorns and bay leaf in a large pan, and season to taste with salt. Bring to the boil and skim. • Lower the heat and poach the chicken for 30 minutes. • Add the bouquet garni and poach for a further 1 hour. Remove the chicken and the giblets, and set aside. Remove the peppercorns, bay leaf and bouquet garni and discard. Rub the chicken stock through a sieve. • Peel and finely chop the onion and garlic. Wash, pat dry and dice the aubergines and courgettes. • Skin and chop the tomatoes. • Heat the oil, and fry the onion and garlic until transparent. Add the aubergines, courgettes and thyme, and fry over a low heat for 10 minutes. • Add 250ml/8fl oz of the reserved stock. • Bring the remaining stock to the boil in a different pan. Add the pasta bows, bring back to the boil and cook rapidly for 5-8 minutes. • Skin the chicken. Dice the meat and add to the vegetables. Add the cooked noodles and stock in which they were cooked, and heat through.

Farmhouse Stew

The rich stock can be used as a basis for sauces and gravies

800g/1½lbs boneless turkey thighs	
1 onion	
2 cloves	
500-750ml/16fl oz-1¼ pints water	
1 bay leaf	
Salt	
2 carrots	
2 leeks	
125ml/4fl oz double cream	
2 tbsps freshly grated horseradish	

Preparation time: 1 hour
Nutritional value:
Analysis per serving, approx:
• 1600kJ/380kcal
• 46g protein
• 16g fat
• 15g carbohydrate

Rinse the turkey thighs and pat dry. Peel the onion and stud with the cloves. • Place the water in a pan and bring to the boil. Add the turkey, onion, cloves and bay leaf, and season to taste with salt. Lower the heat and simmer for 20 minutes. Skim frequently during this time. • Peel and coarsely slice the carrots. Trim, wash and halve the leeks. Cut into 2cm/³/₄-inch chunks. • Add the carrots and leeks to the pan, cover and cook for a further 25 minutes. Discard the onion and bay leaf. • Remove the meat and vegetables with a slotted spoon. Slice the meat and arrange with the vegetables in a tureen. • Whip the cream until fairly thick, and mix with the horseradish. Reserve a small amount of horseradish for the garnish, if liked. Hand the horseradish cream separately. • Rye bread rolls make a tasty accompaniment.

Paella

Travellers to Spain will be familiar with this famous rice dish

To serve 8:

1 x 1.2kg/2½lbs chicken
250g/8oz pork fillet
Salt and freshly ground black pepper
6 tbsps olive oil
500g/1lb 2oz mussels
300g/10oz long-grain rice
2 onions
2 garlic cloves
750ml/1¼ pints chicken stock
125ml/4fl oz dry white wine
½ tsp saffron
100g/4oz shelled peas
200g/7oz smoked garlic sausage or Spanish chorizo
6 cooked king prawns
4 beefsteak tomatoes
1 lemon
100g/4oz black olives

Preparation time: 2 hours
Nutritional value:

Analysis per serving, approx:
• 2625kJ/625kcal

• 51g protein
• 31g fat
• 36g carbohydrate

Rinse the chicken carefully inside and out and pat dry. Cut into 12 pieces. Wash, pat dry and dice the pork. • Season the chicken and pork lightly with salt and pepper to taste. • Heat 4 tbsps of the oil in a large pan, and fry the chicken pieces until golden on all sides. Add the pork, and fry until lightly coloured. Lower the heat and cook the chicken and pork for a further 20 minutes, stirring frequently. • Scrub the mussels under cold running water, discarding any that do not close when sharply tapped. Pull off the beards. • Rinse the rice under cold running water. • Thinly slice the sausage. Add the sausage to the pan, and fry until lightly coloured. • Peel and finely chop the onions and garlic. Heat the remaining oil in another large pan, and fry the onions and garlic until

lightly coloured. Add the rice and fry, stirring constantly, until golden. Pour over the chicken stock and wine. Stir in the saffron. Cook the rice for 10 minutes over a low heat. • Add the peas, and cook for a further 10 minutes. To skin the tomatoes, just drop them into a pan of boiling water for about 1 minute, then place in cold water. Cut a cross in the top of the tomatoes and peel off the skin. Cut the tomatoes into 8. • Transfer the rice to a paella pan or a large, flat, ovenproof dish. Arrange the chicken, pork, mussels, sausage, prawns and tomato wedges on top. • Bake in a preheated oven at 200°C/400°F/gas mark 6 for 20 minutes. • Cut the lemon into wedges. • Switch off the oven and leave the paella to rest for 5 minutes. All the mussels should be opened; discard any that are not. Scatter over the olives. Garnish with the lemon wedges and serve immediately.

Our tip: Paella is made in many different ways in Spain, depending on the region and the availability of ingredients. If you can bring a typical smoked chorizo sausage back from Spain, you can make an authentic paella. Alternatively, experiment with the numerous kinds of sausage that are now finding their way onto our supermarket shelves.

Chicken Stew

A chicken dish from the southern United States, made with kidney beans and sweetcorn

1 x 1.2kg/2¹/₂lbs chicken, with giblets
Salt and freshly ground white pepper
1 onion
3 potatoes
400g/7oz tomatoes
1 x 200g/7oz can kidney beans
1 x 200g/7oz can sweetcorn
1 tsp sugar
2 tbsps snipped chives
1 small bunch of chives (optional)

Preparation time: 45 minutes
Cooking time: 1¹/₂ hours
Nutritional value:
Analysis per serving, approx:
- 2400kJ/570kcal
- 67g protein
- 22g fat
- 33g carbohydrate

Rinse the chicken and pat dry. Cut into 8 pieces. Place the chicken and giblets in a pan, and add enough boiling water just to cover. • Cook over a low heat for 45 minutes. Skim frequently during this time. • Season to taste with salt, cover and simmer for a further 25 minutes. • Peel and slice the onion and push out into rings. Peel and roughly dice the potatoes. Add the onion and the potatoes to the pan, and cook for a further 20 minutes. • Skin the tomatoes and cut into 8. Drain the kidney beans and the sweetcorn. Add the tomatoes, kidney beans and sweetcorn to the pan, and cook for a further 10 minutes. • Remove the chicken from the stew. Skin the chicken and cut the meat from the bones. Dice the meat and return it to the stew. Add the sugar, and season to taste with salt and pepper. Heat through and serve sprinkled with the snipped chives. Garnish with whole chives, if liked.

Caucasian Chicken Casserole

A spicy rice and vegetable treat – the gherkin cream gives it a special piquancy

1 x 1kg/2¼lb chicken
4 tbsps sunflower oil
Salt and freshly ground black pepper
½ tsp mild paprika
1 onion
1 carrot
200g/7oz celery or celeriac
150g/5oz cucumber
150g/5oz pumpkin or courgettes
125g/5oz long-grain rice
1 bay leaf
¼ tsp fennel seeds
1l/1¾ pints water
1 pickled gherkin
4 tbsps soured cream

Preparation time: 30 minutes
Cooking time: 45 minutes
Nutritional value:
Analysis per serving, approx:
- 2400kJ/570kcal
- 56g protein
- 27g fat
- 36g carbohydrate

Rinse the chicken and pat dry. Divide into 4 pieces. • Season 1 tbsp of the oil with salt and pepper, and stir in the paprika. Brush the chicken pieces with the seasoned oil, and set aside to marinate for 10 minutes. • Peel and chop the onion. Peel the carrot. Trim the celery, if using. Peel the celeriac, if using. Peel the cucumber. Peel the pumpkin, if using. Wash the courgettes, if using. Chop all the vegetables into 3cm/1¼-inch chunks. • Heat the remaining oil in a large flameproof casserole, and fry the chicken until golden on all sides. Add the onion, carrot and celery or celeriac, and fry for 1-2 minutes until lightly coloured. • Wash the rice under cold running water. Add the rice, bay leaf and fennel seeds to the pan. Pour over the water, cover and cook over a low heat for 30 minutes. • Add the cucumber and pumpkin or courgettes. Cook, uncovered, in a preheated oven at 240°C/475°F/gas mark 9 for 15 minutes. • Finely chop the pickled gherkin, and stir into the soured cream. • Serve straight from the casserole, and hand the gherkin cream separately.

Pot-Cooked Chicken

An ancient recipe from Lombardy

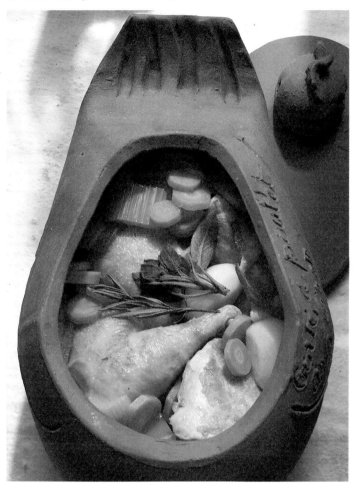

500g/1lb 2oz celery stalks	
400g/7oz carrots	
400g/7oz small potatoes	
1 x 1.2kg/2½lb chicken	
1 tbsp lemon juice	
Salt and freshly ground white pepper	
50g/2oz thinly sliced rindless bacon	
5 tbsps dry white wine	
1 rosemary sprig	
1 sage sprig	
15g/½oz butter	

Preparation time: 25 minutes
Cooking time: 1½ hours
Nutritional value:
Analysis per serving, approx:
• 2700kJ/640kcal
• 68g protein
• 31g fat
• 30g carbohydrate

Soak a clay pot and lid in cold water for about 20 minutes. • Trim and wash the celery. Cut into 3cm/1¼-inch chunks. Peel and slice the carrots. Peel and quarter the potatoes. • Divide the chicken into 8 pieces. Wash, dry and sprinkle with the lemon juice. • Rub in a little salt and pepper. • Remove the clay pot from the water, and line with the bacon. Cover with half the vegetables. Season lightly with salt and pepper. Place the chicken pieces on top. Cover with the remaining vegetables, and again season lightly with salt and pepper. • Pour over the wine. Wash and pat dry the rosemary and sage and place on top of the vegetables. • Cover the pot and place on the lowest shelf of a cold oven. Set the oven to 220°C/425°F/gas mark 7, and cook the chicken for 1 hour 20 minutes. • Remove the lid, return the pot to the oven and cook for a further 10 minutes. Dot with the butter and serve.

Asparagus and Chicken Casserole

A light meal for the asparagus season, with new potatoes

1.5kg/3lbs 6oz asparagus	
2l/3½ pints water	
Salt and freshly ground white pepper	
500g/1lb 2oz skinless chicken fillets	
25g/1oz butter	
2 tbsps flour	
125ml/4fl oz milk	
1 egg yolk	
5 tbsps crème fraîche	
2 tbsps snipped chives	

Preparation time: 1 hour
Nutritional value:
Analysis per serving, approx:
• 1500kJ/360kcal
• 38g protein
• 17g fat
• 17g carbohydrate

Peel the asparagus. Bring the water to the boil with 1 tsp salt. Add the asparagus, and cook for 15 minutes until tender. • Wash, pat dry and dice the chicken fillets. Melt half the butter, and stir-fry the chicken for 6 minutes. Remove the chicken from the pan. • Drain the asparagus, and reserve 250ml/8fl oz of the cooking liquid. • Melt the remaining butter, and stir in the flour. Cook, stirring constantly, for 3 minutes or until golden. Gradually stir in the milk and the reserved cooking liquid, and bring to the boil, stirring constantly. Lower the heat, season to taste with salt and pepper and simmer, stirring constantly, for 10 minutes. • Cut the asparagus into 4cm/1½-inch chunks. Add the asparagus and chicken to the sauce. • Beat together the egg yolk and crème fraîche, and stir into the pan. Remove the stew from the heat and sprinkle with the chives. Serve with new potatoes.

Western and Eastern Specialities

These substantial vegetable hot-pots with chicken or goose drumsticks are known as Garbure and Solyanka in their native countries

Béarnaise Vegetable Hot-pot
Illustrated left

| 2 x 600g/1¼lb goose drumsticks |
| 1l/1¾ pints water |
| Salt and freshly ground white pepper |
| 1 onion |
| ½ bay leaf • 100g/4oz carrots |
| 200g/7oz white turnip |
| 200g/7oz potatoes |
| 200g/7oz white cabbage |
| 200g/7oz French beans |
| 150g/5oz canned butter beans |
| 2 chervil sprigs • 1 lovage sprig |
| 4 tbsps freshly grated Parmesan cheese |
| 1 tbsp finely chopped fresh parsley |

Preparation time: 30 minutes
Cooking time: 1 hour 50 minutes
Nutritional value:
Analysis per serving, approx:

- 2100kJ/500kcal • 71g protein
- 13g fat • 25g carbohydrate

Wash the goose drumsticks. Place the drumsticks and water in a pan, season to taste with salt and bring to the boil. Peel the onion. Add the onion and bay leaf to the pan. Lower the heat, and simmer for 20 minutes. Skim frequently during this time. • Cover the pan, and cook for a further 1 hour. • Peel and dice the carrots. Peel and dice the turnip. Peel and roughly dice the potatoes. • Trim, wash and shred the cabbage. Wash and slice the French beans. Drain the butter beans. • Add the carrots, turnip, potatoes, cabbage, French beans, butter beans, chervil and lovage to the pan, cover and cook for a further 30 minutes. • Remove the drumsticks from the pan. Skin and cut the meat from the bones. Dice the meat and return it to the pan. Heat through and serve sprinkled with the Parmesan cheese and parsley.

Solyanka
Illustrated right

| 1 x 1.2kg/2½lb chicken, with giblets |
| 2 red peppers |
| 1.5l/2½ pints water |
| Salt and freshly ground white pepper |
| 1 onion • 1 bouquet garni |
| 600g/1¼lbs white cabbage |
| 2 pickled gherkins |
| 125ml/4fl oz dry white wine |
| 6 tbsps crème fraîche |
| 3 tbsps finely chopped fresh dill |

Preparation time: 30 minutes
Cooking time: 2 hours
Nutritional value:
Analysis per serving, approx:
- 2300kJ/550kcal • 65g protein
- 29g fat • 11g carbohydrate

Wash the chicken and the giblets. • Halve, seed, wash and coarsely chop the peppers. Place the water and peppers in a pan, and season to taste with salt. Bring the water to the boil. • Peel and halve the onion. Add the chicken, giblets, onion and bouquet garni to the pan, lower the heat and cook for 30 minutes. Skim frequently during this time. • Partially cover the pan, and cook for a further 1 hour. • Remove the onion and the bouquet garni and discard. • Trim the cabbage and discard the stalk and any tough outer leaves. Wash and shred the cabbage. Cut the pickled gherkins into matchstick strips. Add the cabbage and the gherkins to the pan, cover and cook for a further 10 minutes. • Remove the chicken and the giblets from the stock. Discard the giblets. Skin the chicken and cut the meat from the bones. Dice the meat. • Boil the stock uncovered until reduced by half. • Return the chicken meat to the pan, add the wine and season to taste. Stir in the crème fraîche. Serve sprinkled with the dill.

Creole Rice

This substantial dish is very similar to Jambalaya, a recipe from the southern United States

To serve 8:

200g/7 oz pork fillet
1 x 1.2kg/2¹/₂lbs chicken
Salt and freshly ground white pepper
5 tbsps sunflower oil
2 onions
1 garlic clove
2 green peppers
1 red pepper
2 beefsteak tomatoes
750ml/1¹/₄ pints hot chicken stock
250g/8oz long-grain rice
¹/₄ tsp cayenne
¹/₄ tsp saffron
200g/7oz garlic sausage
200g/7oz lean ham
200g/7oz lobster meat

Preparation time: 45 minutes
Cooking time: 55 minutes
Nutritional value:
Analysis per serving, approx:
• 2300kJ/550kcal • 49g protein
• 35g fat • 20g carbohydrate

Rinse the pork and the chicken and pat dry. Cut the chicken into 8 pieces. Dice the pork. Place the meat in a large, shallow dish. • Mix together 1 tsp salt, a pinch of pepper and the oil. Pour over the chicken and pork, cover and set aside to marinate for 30 minutes. • Peel and finely chop the onions. Peel and finely chop the garlic. Halve, core and seed the peppers. Wash, dry and dice them. Skin the tomatoes and cut into 8. • Heat a large flameproof casserole over a low heat, add the chicken, pork and the marinade. Cook, stirring frequently until lightly browned on all sides. Add the onions, garlic and peppers, and cook, stirring frequently, until lightly coloured. Pour in half the stock, bring to the boil and lower the heat. Cover and cook for 30 minutes. Wash the rice under cold running water. • Add the tomatoes, rice, remaining stock, cayenne and saffron to the casserole, cover, and cook for a further 20 minutes. • Slice the sausage. Cut the ham and lobster meat into strips. Place on top of the stew and heat through for 5 minutes.

Chicken Pot-au-feu

This classic dish is usually made with beef – here is a variation using chicken

1 x 1.2kg/2¹/₂lb chicken, with giblets

750ml/1¹/₄ pints chicken stock

100g/4oz carrots

200g/7oz leeks

1 onion

500g/1lb 2oz pickled cabbage

1 bay leaf

4 juniper berries

400g/14oz tomatoes

Salt and freshly ground black pepper

Preparation time: 35 minutes
Cooking time: 1 hour
Nutritional value:
Analysis per serving, approx:
• 2100kJ/500kcal
• 67g protein
• 21g fat
• 17g carbohydrate

Wash and pat dry the chicken, the heart and the liver, and discard the rest of the giblets. Divide the chicken into 8 pieces. • Place the chicken stock in a large flameproof casserole, and bring to the boil. Add the chicken pieces and the heart, reduce the heat and cook for 30 minutes. Skim frequently during this time. • Peel and dice the carrots. Trim, halve and wash the leeks, and cut into 5cm/2-inch chunks. Peel and slice the onion and push out into rings. Coarsely shred the pickled cabbage. Slice the chicken liver. • Add the carrots, leeks, onion, pickled cabbage, bay leaf, juniper berries and the chicken liver to the casserole, cover and cook for a further 20 minutes. • Skin the tomatoes and cut into 8. Add to the casserole, and season to taste with salt and pepper. Cook for a further 10 minutes. • Serve straight from the casserole. Freshly baked French bread makes an excellent accompaniment.

Chicken Drumsticks with Lentils

An unusual but tasty mixture

500g/1lb 2oz brown lentils
1.5l/2¹/₂ pints water
250 ml/8fl oz dry red wine
4 x 200g/7 oz chicken drumsticks
2 tbsps chicken stock granules
1 bay leaf
1 dried chilli
¹/₂ tsp dried thyme
1 tsp dried basil
Salt and freshly ground white pepper
100g/4oz rindless streaky bacon
1 tbsp sunflower oil
2 onions
1 garlic clove
Pinch of sugar
1 parsley sprig

Preparation time: 25 minutes
Cooking time: 45 minutes
Nutritional value:
Analysis per serving, approx:
• 3700kJ/880kcal
• 74g protein
• 26g fat
• 75g carbohydrate

Wash the lentils. Place in a pan, cover with water, add the wine and bring to the boil. • Rinse the chicken drumsticks. Add the drumsticks, stock granules, bay leaf, chilli, thyme and basil to the pan, and season to taste with pepper. Bring back to the boil, lower the heat, cover, and cook for 45 minutes. • Finely dice the bacon. Heat the oil, and fry the bacon until the fat runs. Peel and slice the onions and push out into rings. Add to the pan, and fry until golden brown. • Peel and crush the garlic. Add to the pan, and fry gently until lightly coloured. • Transfer the lentil and chicken mixture to a serving dish. Top with the bacon, onion and garlic mixture • Sprinkle over the sugar, and season to taste with salt. Garnish with the parsley sprig.

Chicken Liver Pilaf

A change from the well-known lamb pilaf

250g/8oz long-grain rice
750ml/1¹/₄ pints water
Salt and freshly ground white pepper
500g/1lb 2oz chicken livers
2 red peppers
1 onion
50g/2oz butter
125ml/4fl oz vegetable stock
4 tbsps white wine
4 tbsps crème fraîche
1 tbsp finely chopped fresh parsley

Preparation time: 45 minutes
Nutritional value:
Analysis per serving, approx:
• 2100kJ/500kcal
• 34g protein
•16g fat
• 58g carbohydrate

Wash the rice under cold running water. Place the water in a pan, add salt to taste and bring to the boil. Add the rice, lower the heat, cover and cook for 20 minutes. • Wash the chicken livers, pat dry and dice. Halve, core and seed the peppers. Wash, pat dry and finely dice. Peel and finely chop the onion. • Melt half the butter in a large flameproof casserole, and gently fry the chicken livers for 4 minutes, stirring frequently. Remove from the pan and keep warm. • Melt the remaining butter in the casserole, and gently fry the onion until transparent. Add the peppers, and fry for a further 10 minutes, stirring frequently. Add the stock and bring to the boil. Lower the heat, cover and simmer for a further 10 minutes. • Stir in the rice, wine and chicken livers. Season to taste with salt and pepper, and stir in the crème fraîche and the parsley.

Braised Dishes and Ragouts

Specialities from Coq au vin
to Szechwan chicken

Coq au Vin

One of the most famous French recipes

1 x 1.5kg /3lb 6oz chicken
Salt and freshly ground white pepper
100g/4oz rindless streaky bacon
8 small onions
1 garlic clove
2 carrots
25g/1oz butter
1 bay leaf
1 thyme sprig
750ml/1¼ pints dry red wine
150g/5oz mushrooms
1 tsp cornflour
2 tbsps brandy
3 tbsps finely chopped fresh flat-leafed parsley

Preparation time: 50 minutes
Cooking time: 50 minutes
Nutritional value:

Analysis per serving, approx:
• 3900kJ/930kcal • 83g protein
• 47g fat • 18g carbohydrate

Wash the chicken and pat dry. Cut into 8 pieces, and season to taste with salt and pepper. • Finely dice the bacon. Peel and chop the onions and garlic. Peel and dice the carrots. • Melt the butter in a flameproof casserole, and fry the chicken and bacon until golden on all sides. Add the onion, garlic and carrots, and fry for 5 minutes. • Add the bay leaf, thyme and wine. Cover and braise the chicken for 40 minutes. • Trim, wipe and dice the mushrooms. • Transfer the chicken and bacon to a serving dish and keep warm. Strain the cooking juices and return to the casserole. Add the mushrooms, and cook over a low heat for 10 minutes. • Mix the cornflour with a little water to make a paste. Stir the paste into the sauce and cook, stirring constantly, until thickened. Season to taste with salt, and stir in the brandy. Pour the sauce over the chicken and sprinkle with the parsley.

Chicken in White Wine Sauce

Serve with the same wine

1 x 1.5kg/3lb 6oz chicken
150g/5oz shallots
250ml/8fl oz water
Salt and freshly ground white pepper
2 garlic cloves
80g/3½oz butter
3 tbsps finely chopped fresh tarragon
2 tbsps finely chopped fresh parsley
500ml/16fl oz medium dry white wine
200g/7oz mushrooms
½ tsp flour
200ml/7fl oz crème fraîche

Preparation time: 30 minutes
Cooking time: 35 minutes
Nutritional value:

Analysis per serving, approx:
• 4100kJ/980kcal • 81g protein
• 62g fat • 12g carbohydrate

Cut the wings from the chicken. Peel and quarter the shallots. Place 1 shallot, the chicken wings, water and a pinch of salt in a pan. Bring to the boil, lower the heat and simmer for 20 minutes. Strain and reserve the stock. • Wash the remaining chicken and pat dry. Cut into 8 pieces. Peel and chop the garlic. • Melt half the butter, and fry the chicken until golden on all sides. Add the remaining shallots, garlic, tarragon, parsley, wine and reserved stock, and season to taste with salt and pepper. Cover and cook over a low heat for 25 minutes. • Wipe and thinly slice the mushrooms. Sprinkle over the flour. Melt the remaining butter, and fry the mushrooms for 10 minutes. • Uncover the chicken, increase the heat to high and cook for a further 10 minutes. • Transfer the chicken pieces to a serving dish and keep them warm. • Stir the crème fraîche and mushrooms into the sauce. Season to taste with salt and pepper, and pour the sauce over the chicken.

Delicate Variations on Turkey Roll

Lean turkey pieces make tasty ingredients for light meals

Turkey Roll with Soft Cheese
Illustrated left

2 carrots • 1 small onion

40g/1¹/₂ oz butter • 2 tbsps finely chopped fresh mixed herbs

100g/4oz full-fat soft cheese

1 egg yolk • 1 tbsp French mustard • Salt and freshly ground white pepper

2 x150g/5oz turkey escalopes

250ml/8fl oz hot chicken stock

4 tbsps dry vermouth

2 tbsps crème fraîche

Preparation time: 30 minutes
Cooking time: 20 minutes
Nutritional value:
Analysis per serving, approx:
• 1600kJ/380kcal • 39g protein
• 22g fat • 7g carbohydrate

Peel the carrots and cut into matchstick strips. Peel and finely chop the onion. • Melt 15g/¹/₂oz of the butter, and fry the carrot and onion over a low heat for 5 minutes. Set aside to cool slightly. • Mix together the herbs, cheese, egg yolk and mustard, and season to taste with salt and pepper. • Wash the turkey and pat dry. Spread the cheese and herb mixture evenly over the escalopes. Divide the onion and carrots between them. Roll up the escalopes and secure with wooden cocktail sticks. • Melt the remaining butter, and fry the escalopes over a medium heat until browned on all sides. Pour over the stock and vermouth. Cover and cook over a low heat for 20 minutes. • Transfer the turkey rolls to a carving dish or chopping board and remove the cocktail sticks. Cut the rolls into slices, transfer to a serving dish and keep warm. • Stir the crème fraîche into the cooking juices and heat through. Serve the turkey with new potatoes and carrots and hand the sauce separately.

Turkey Rolls with Vegetables
Illustrated right

50g/2oz raisins

100g/4oz raw ham

1 onion

3 tbsps finely chopped fresh parsley

2 tbsps pine nuts

1 tbsp capers

4 x 150g/5oz turkey escalopes

Salt and freshly ground white pepper

4 tbsps olive oil

4 tbsps tomato purée

125ml/4fl oz water

200ml/7fl oz single cream

1 small bay leaf

1 tsp finely chopped fresh rosemary • ¹/₂ tsp dried thyme

1 red pepper • Pinch of sugar

Preparation time: 45 minutes
Nutritional value:
Analysis per serving, approx:
• 2400kJ/570kcal • 42g protein
• 37g fat • 16g carbohydrate

Place the raisins in a small pan. Cover with water and bring to the boil. Drain. • Dice the ham. Peel and finely chop the onion. • Mix together the raisins, ham, parsley, pine nuts and capers. • Wash the turkey escalopes and pat dry. Season to taste with salt and pepper. Divide the ham and raisin mixture between the escalopes, roll up and secure with wooden cocktail sticks. • Heat the oil, and fry the onion and turkey rolls until the rolls are browned on all sides. Add the tomato purée, water, cream, bay leaf, rosemary and thyme. Cover and cook over a low heat for 20 minutes. • Halve, seed and wash the pepper. Cut into strips. Add to the pan, and cook for a further 10 minutes. Stir in the sugar. • Transfer to a serving dish, remove the cocktail sticks and serve immediately.

43

Tasty Turkey Portions

Tender turkey meat and turkey liver do not take long to cook – just the thing for quick and tasty meals

Hungarian Turkey Ragout
Illustrated left

500g/1lb 2oz turkey breast	
1 onion	
250g/8oz mushrooms	
1 tbsp lemon juice	
2 tbsps sunflower oil	
15g/¹/₂ oz butter	
1 tsp cornflour	
1 tsp mild paprika	
125ml/4fl oz crème fraîche	
125ml/4fl oz dry white wine	
Salt and freshly ground white pepper	

Preparation time: 30 minutes
Nutritional value:
Analysis per serving, approx:
• 1400kJ/330kcal
• 31g protein
• 18g fat
• 7g carbohydrate

Wash the turkey breast and pat dry. Cut into thin slices. Peel and finely chop the onion. Thinly slice the mushrooms, and sprinkle with the lemon juice. • Heat the oil in a large pan, and stir-fry the turkey until brown on all sides. Remove from the pan with a slotted spoon and set aside. • Add the butter to the pan and melt. Fry the onion until transparent. Add the mushrooms, cover, and cook over a low heat for 10 minutes. • Mix together the cornflour, paprika and crème fraîche. Return the turkey to the pan, and stir in the crème fraîche mixture. Add the wine, and cook over a low heat for a few minutes. Season to taste with salt and pepper. • Transfer to a serving dish, and serve with potato croquettes or noodles and a crispy green salad.

Turkey Livers on a Bed of Banana Rice
Illustrated right

200g/7oz long-grain rice	
2¹/₂ ¹/₄ pints water	
Salt and freshly ground white pepper	
100g/4oz shallots	
600g/1¹/₄ lbs turkey livers	
1 tbsp flour	
40g/1¹/₂ oz butter	
3 tbsps curry powder	
50g/2oz chopped almonds	
125ml/4fl oz cream	
125ml/4fl oz chicken stock	
2 small bananas	
1 tsp lemon juice	

Preparation time: 35 minutes
Nutritional value:
Analysis per serving, approx:
• 2700kJ/640kcal • 41g protein
• 28g fat • 60g carbohydrate

Wash the rice under cold running water. • Bring the water to the boil. Add ¹/₂ tsp salt and the rice, and boil for 20 minutes. • Peel and finely chop the shallots. • Wash the livers and pat dry. Cut into bite-sized pieces and toss in the flour. • Melt 25g/1oz of the butter, and fry the shallots until transparent. Add the livers, and stir-fry for 5 minutes. Stir in 2 tbsps of the curry powder and the almonds. Gradually stir in the cream and stock, and simmer for 5 minutes. Season to taste with salt and pepper. • Drain the rice. • Peel and slice the bananas. Melt the remaining butter in another pan, and fry the bananas, stirring frequently, until light brown. Stir in the remaining curry powder, the rice and lemon juice. • Serve the banana rice with the ragout.

Chicken Livers with Lentils

Tasty and colourful

1l/1³/₄ pints water
350g/11oz red lentils
100g/4oz raw ham
500g/1lb 2oz chicken livers
50g/2oz butter
1 tbsp olive oil
3 tbsps finely chopped fresh parsley
1 tbsps finely chopped fresh sage
3 tbsps chicken stock
Salt and freshly ground black pepper
1 sage sprig

Preparation time: 40 minutes
Nutritional value:
Analysis per serving, approx:
• 1800kJ/430kcal
• 38g protein
• 25g fat
• 13g carbohydrate

Bring the water to the boil. Add the lentils, and cook over a low heat for 8 minutes. Drain. • Finely dice the ham. Wash the chicken livers and pat dry. Trim and cut into strips. • Melt half the butter with the oil in a pan, and fry the ham, parsley and sage over a low heat, stirring constantly, for 5 minutes. Add the stock, cover, and cook for a further 5 minutes. • Melt the remaining butter in another pan, and stir-fry the chicken livers for 3-4 minutes. Season to taste with salt and pepper. Mix together the lentils, ham mixture and chicken livers. Transfer to a serving dish and garnish with the sage leaves. Serve immediately. • Mashed potato or freshly baked baguette make an excellent accompaniment.

Chicken Livers with Yogurt Sauce

Economical and full of protein

2 tbsps finely chopped fresh parsley
2 tbsps torn fresh basil leaves
2 tbsps snipped chives
300ml/10fl oz natural yogurt
4 tbsps double cream
1 tsp lemon juice
1 garlic clove
Salt and freshly ground black pepper
¹/₄ tsp sugar
500g/1lb 2oz chicken livers
1 tbsp flour
2 onions
3 tbsps corn oil
¹/₂ tsp dried mixed herbs

Preparation time: 35 minutes
Nutritional value:
Analysis per serving, approx:
• 1400kJ/330kcal
• 32g protein
• 18g fat
• 12g carbohydrate

Mix together the parsley, basil, chives, yogurt, cream and lemon juice. Peel and chop the garlic. Sprinkle with the salt, crush and add to the yogurt sauce. Stir in the sugar, and season to taste with pepper. • Trim the chicken livers, wash and pat dry. Toss in the flour to coat thoroughly. • Peel and thinly slice the onions and push out into rings. • Heat 1 tbsp of the oil in a frying pan, and fry the onions for 5 minutes. Remove from the pan. • Add the remaining oil to the pan, and stir-fry the livers for about 2 minutes. Return the onions to the pan, and fry for a further 1 minute. Sprinkle over the dried herbs and season to taste with salt and pepper. • Transfer to a serving dish and hand the yogurt sauce separately.

Chicken Hearts with Vegetables

Chicken heart contains no cholesterol

Turkey Livers with Tomatoes

Turkey liver is rich in minerals

1kg/2¼ lbs chicken hearts
1 onion
2 celery stalks
250g/8oz small carrots
250g/8oz shallots
250g/8oz potatoes
4 tbsps olive oil
125ml/4fl oz dry white wine
250ml/8fl oz chicken stock
Salt and freshly ground black pepper
3 tbsps finely chopped fresh parsley

Preparation time: 1 hour
Cooking time: 15 minutes
Nutritional value:

Analysis per serving, approx:
- 2200kJ/520kcal
- 48g protein
- 22g fat
- 31g carbohydrate

Trim the chicken hearts, cut in half, wash and pat dry. • Peel and coarsely chop the onion.

Trim, wash and chop the celery. Peel and slice the carrots. Peel and chop the shallots. Peel and dice the potatoes. • Heat 3 tbsps of the oil and fry the onion until transparent. Add the chicken hearts, and fry until they begin to colour. Add the wine and cook, stirring constantly, until it has evaporated. • Stir in the celery, carrots, shallots, potatoes and stock, and season to taste with salt and pepper. Cover and simmer for 15 minutes or until the meat is tender. • Stir in the remaining oil. Transfer to a serving dish and sprinkle over the parsley.

2 large onions
2 beefsteak tomatoes
50g/2oz butter
100ml/3½fl oz dry white wine
500g/1lb 2oz turkey livers
1 tbsp flour
2 sage sprigs
Salt and freshly ground black pepper

Preparation time: 40 minutes
Nutritional value:

Analysis per serving, approx:
- 1300kJ/310kcal
- 30g protein
- 15g fat
- 12g carbohydrate

Peel and thinly slice the onions and push out into rings. Skin the tomatoes and cut into wedges. • Melt half the butter, and fry the onion until golden brown. Add the wine, cover, and cook for about 5 minutes. • Add the tomatoes, and cook over a medium heat for 5 minutes or until the liquid has

reduced a little. • Trim the turkey livers, wash and pat dry. Cut into strips and coat with the flour. • Wash the sage and pat dry. • Melt the remaining butter in another pan, and fry the livers until they are beginning to colour. • Stir the liver into the tomato sauce, and season to taste with salt and pepper. Transfer to a serving dish and serve immediately. • Parsley potatoes make an excellent accompaniment.

Our tip: If chicken stock is added to the sauce, brown rice can also be mixed into the ragout.

Chicken Liver with Celery

Fresh chicken livers are best used on the day of purchase

750g/1½ lbs chicken livers
1 tbsp flour
3 tbsps olive oil
1 onion
1 x 400g/14oz can peeled tomatoes
2 large beefsteak tomatoes
600g/1¼ lbs celery
Salt and freshly ground white pepper
1 tsp dried oregano
4 lemon balm sprigs
100g/4oz shelled walnuts
125ml/4fl oz crème fraîche

Preparation time: 1 hour
Nutritional value:
Analysis per serving, approx:
- 2800kJ/670kcal
- 50g protein
- 43g fat
- 22g carbohydrate

Trim the livers, wash and pat dry. Cut into bite-sized pieces and dredge with the flour. • Heat the oil, and stir-fry the livers until well browned. Remove from the pan and set aside. • Peel and finely chop the onion. Fry in the same pan until transparent. • Drain the canned tomatoes, and mash to make a rough purée. Add the purée to the pan, and cook over a medium heat until slightly thickened. • Skin the beefsteak tomatoes and cut into wedges. • Trim and wash the celery. Cut into 2cm/¾-inch pieces. Add the celery and tomato wedges to the pan, cover and cook for 15 minutes. Season to taste with salt and pepper, and stir in the oregano. • Wash the lemon balm sprigs and pat dry. Separate the leaves. Chop the walnuts. • Stir the walnuts and crème fraîche into the pan, and heat through. Transfer to a serving dish and sprinkle with the lemon balm leaves. • This is particularly tasty served with mashed potato.

Delicious Ways with Chicken Breast Fillets

The side-dishes and seasoning that go with these fricassées are reminiscent of oriental cuisine

Chicken Curry
Illustrated left

500g/1lb 2oz chicken breast fillets	
1/2 bunch spring onions	
1 large beefsteak tomato	
1/2 pineapple	
25g/1oz butter	
1 tsp flour	
2 tbsps curry powder	
250ml/8fl oz chicken stock	
1 tsp lemon juice	
Salt	

Preparation time: 30 minutes
Nutritional value:
Analysis per serving, approx:
• 1100kJ/260kcal
• 30g protein
• 7g fat
• 21g carbohydrate

Wash the chicken and pat dry. Cut into strips about 1cm/1/2 inch wide. • Trim and wash the spring onions. Cut the pale green parts into 1cm/1/2-inch rings. Cut the white ends lengthways into quarters. • Skin and dice the tomato. • Peel, quarter, core and slice the pineapple • Melt the butter, and fry the chicken until golden brown. Add the onions and tomato, and fry for a further 1 minute. • Mix together the flour and curry powder, and stir into the pan. Gradually stir in the stock. • Add the pineapple, and simmer over a low heat for 5 minutes. Stir in the lemon juice and season to taste with salt. • This fruity curry may be served with brown rice.

Chicken Breast with Walnuts
Illustrated right

500g/1lb 2oz chicken breast fillets	
3 tbsps soya sauce	
2 tbsps dry sherry	
1/2 tsp sugar	
2 tbsps cornflour	
Salt	
1 red pepper	
1 onion	
200g/7oz celery	
5 tbsps corn oil	
100g/4oz shelled walnuts	
125ml/4fl oz hot chicken stock	

Preparation time: 35 minutes
Nutritional value:
Analysis per serving, approx:
• 1800kJ/430kcal
• 34g protein
• 25g fat
• 14g carbohydrate

Wash the chicken and pat dry. Cut into 2cm/3/4-inch cubes, and place in a shallow dish. • Mix together the soya sauce, sherry, sugar and cornflour, and season to taste with salt. Pour the mixture over the chicken. • Halve, seed and wash the pepper and cut into matchstick strips. Peel the onion and cut into matchstick strips. Trim and wash the celery and cut into matchstick strips. • Heat 1 tbsp of the oil, and fry the walnuts until pale brown. Remove from the pan. • Add 1 tbsp of the remaining oil, and stir-fry the celery for 1 minute. Add the onion, and stir-fry for 1 minute. Add the pepper, and stir-fry for 1 minute. Remove the vegetables from the pan. • Heat the remaining oil, and stir-fry the chicken for 3 minutes. Lower the heat and add the stock. Return the vegetables and walnuts to the pan and heat through. • Transfer to a serving dish and serve with rice.

Exquisite Fricassées

Fricassées can be made from a wide variety of ingredients

Light Chicken Fricassée
Illustrated left

| 1 x 1.5kg/3lb 6oz chicken |
| 2 onions • 1 bouquet garni |
| 1 bay leaf |
| 1 tsp black peppercorns |
| 1l/1¾ pints water |
| Salt and freshly ground white pepper • 50g/2oz butter |
| 125ml/4fl oz dry white wine |
| 250ml/8fl oz double cream |
| 100g/4oz crème fraîche |
| 200g/7oz carrots |
| 150g/5oz celery • 1 small leek |
| ½ tsp dried tarragon |
| 1 tbsp finely chopped fresh parsley |

Preparation time: 30 minutes
Cooking time: 1 hour
Nutritional value:
Analysis per serving, approx:
• 3200kJ/760kcal • 58g protein
• 49g fat • 21g carbohydrate

Separate the drumsticks and breast from the chicken. Thinly slice and set aside. Cut the remaining parts into several pieces. Peel the onions and finely chop 1, leaving the other whole. • Place the chicken pieces, but not the breast and drumsticks, in a pan, and add the bouquet garni, bay leaf, the whole onion, peppercorns and water, and season to taste with salt. Bring to the boil, lower the heat and simmer for 30 minutes. The liquid should reduce by about one quarter. • Rub the chicken stock through a sieve and reserve. (Use the meat in another recipe.) • Wash the chicken breast and drumsticks and pat dry. Halve and rub with the pepper. Melt the butter, and fry the breast and drumsticks until golden brown. Add the remaining onion, and fry for 5 minutes. Add the chicken stock and wine, and cook for 30 minutes. The liquid should reduce by half. • Stir in the cream and

crème fraîche, and reduce by half.
• Peel the carrots and cut into matchstick strips. Trim and wash the celery and cut into matchstick strips. Trim, halve and wash the leek and cut into matchstick strips.
• Stir the carrots, celery, leek, tarragon and parsley into the pan, and simmer for 3 minutes.

Chicken Fricassée with Millet
Illustrated right

| 1 x 1kg/2¼ lbs chicken |
| Salt and freshly ground white pepper • 1 small bay leaf |
| 5 white peppercorns |
| 1 tbsp dried mixed herbs |
| 1 carrot • 200g/7oz millet |
| 500g/1lb 2oz leeks |
| 40g/1½ oz butter |
| 125ml/4fl oz cream |
| 2 tbsps finely chopped fresh parsley • Juice of ½ lemon |

Preparation time: 30 minutes
Cooking time: 1 hour
Nutritional value:
Analysis per serving, approx:
• 2900kJ/690kcal • 61g protein
• 34g fat • 46g carbohydrate

Wash the chicken. Place in a large pan, cover with water and add a pinch of salt, the bay leaf, peppercorns and mixed herbs. Bring to the boil, lower the heat and simmer for 1 hour. • Remove the chicken and set aside. Rub the stock through a sieve, and reserve 750ml/1¼ pints. • Peel and dice the carrot. Place the carrot, millet and reserved stock in a pan, cover and cook over a low heat for 30 minutes. • Trim, halve and wash the leeks and cut into strips. Melt the butter, and gently fry the leeks for 10 minutes. • Skin the chicken, cut the meat from the bones and cut into pieces. Mix together the chicken, millet, leeks, cream, parsley and lemon juice, and season to taste.

Chicken Marengo

This dish was created by Dunand, Napoleon's chef, following the Battle of Marengo

1 x 1.2kg/2½ lb chicken

Freshly ground white pepper

125ml/4fl oz olive oil

200g/7oz mushrooms

Juice of 1 lemon

6 anchovy fillets

2 garlic cloves

1 sprig parsley

2 sprigs thyme

½ bay leaf

250ml/8fl oz hot chicken stock

400g/14oz tomatoes

12 black olives

2 hard-boiled eggs

Preparation time: 1 hour
Nutritional value:
Analysis per serving, approx:
• 2600kJ/620kcal
• 63g protein
• 41g fat
• 7g carbohydrate

Wash the chicken and pat dry. Cut into 8 portions, and rub with pepper and a little olive oil. • Slice the mushrooms, and sprinkle with the lemon juice. • Finely dice the anchovy fillets. Peel and chop the garlic. Wash the parsley and thyme sprigs and shake dry. Tie the sprigs and the bay leaf together. • Heat the remaining oil, and fry the chicken pieces until golden brown on all sides. Add the mushrooms, anchovies, garlic, herbs and stock, cover and cook over a medium heat for a further 20 minutes. • Skin the tomatoes and cut into wedges. Add the tomatoes and olives to the pan, and cook for a further 5 minutes. • Shell and finely chop the eggs. • Transfer the chicken and vegetables to a serving dish and sprinkle over the eggs.

Braised Peppered Chicken

Chicken goes well with peppers

1 x 1.2kg/2¹/₂ lb chicken
2 onions
2 red peppers
2 green peppers
40g/1¹/₂ oz butter
6 tbsps chicken stock
125ml/4fl oz sour cream
1 tbsp sweet paprika
Salt and freshly ground white pepper
1 tbsp finely chopped fresh parsley

Preparation time: 50 minutes
Nutritional value:
Analysis per serving, approx:
• 2000kJ/480kcal
• 55g protein
• 28g fat
• 11g carbohydrate

Wash the chicken and pat dry. Cut into 8 portions. • Peel and finely chop the onions. Halve, seed and wash the peppers and cut into strips about 3cm/1¹/₂ inches long. • Melt the butter, and fry the onion until transparent. • Add the chicken pieces, and fry, turning frequently, until lightly browned on all sides. Add the peppers and the stock. Cover and cook over a low heat for 30 minutes. • Mix together the sour cream and paprika, and season to taste with salt and pepper. Stir the sour cream mixture into the pan, and cook for a further 5 minutes. • Transfer to a serving dish, sprinkle with the parsley and serve with brown rice.

Chicken Béarnaise

A substantial, satisfying dish

1 x 1.2kg/2¹/₂ lb chicken
1 thick slice stale bread, crusts removed • 150g/5oz cooked ham
1 garlic clove
200g/7oz sausagemeat
2 tbsps snipped chives
1l/1³/₄ pints water • Salt
1 thyme sprig
2 flat-leafed parsley sprigs
1 bay leaf • 1 small onion
2 small carrots
1 celery stalk or 1 small piece celeriac • 2 small leeks
400g/14oz savoy cabbage
200g/7oz French beans

Preparation time: 40 minutes
Cooking time: 1¹/₂ hours
Nutritional value:
Analysis per serving, approx:
• 3200kJ/760kcal • 70g protein
• 47g fat • 22g carbohydrate

Wash the chicken and pat dry. Wash the giblets, if using, and pat dry. • Tear the bread into pieces, place in a small bowl and cover with cold water. Set aside to soak. • Dice the ham and the giblets, if using. Peel and chop the garlic. Squeeze the water from the bread. • Mix together the ham, giblets, sausagemeat, chives, garlic and bread. Spoon the stuffing into the chicken, and close the cavity with wooden cocktail sticks. • Bring the water to the boil, and add a little salt, the thyme, parsley and bay leaf. Add the chicken, cover, and cook over a low heat for 1 hour. • Peel and chop the onion. Peel and slice the carrots. Trim, wash and chop the celery, if using. Peel and chop the celeriac, if using. Trim, wash and slice the leeks. Wash and shred the cabbage. Trim, wash and chop the beans. • Add the onion, carrots, celery or celeriac, leeks, cabbage and beans to the pan, and cook for a further 30 minutes. • Discard the thyme, parsley and bay leaf and remove the cocktail sticks from the chicken before serving.

Braised Chicken with Rosemary

The rosemary gives this dish a Mediterranean character

1 x 1.2kg/2½lb chicken, with giblets
Salt and freshly ground white pepper
25g/1oz butter
125ml/4fl oz chicken stock
1 rosemary sprig
1 small cooking apple
1 small floury potato
125ml/4fl oz dry white wine

Preparation time: 1 hour
Nutritional value:
Analysis per serving, approx:
• 1800kJ/430kcal
• 52g protein
• 22g fat
• 8g carbohydrate

Wash the chicken and pat dry. Cut into 8 portions, and rub with salt. Wash the giblets and pat dry. • Melt the butter in a flameproof casserole, and fry the chicken until browned all over. Add the stock, chicken heart and rosemary, cover, and cook over a low heat for 30 minutes. • Meanwhile, chop the liver. Peel and grate the apple. Peel and grate the potato. • Add the apple, potato, chicken liver and wine to the casserole. If necessary, add a little more stock. Cover and cook for a further 10 minutes. Season to taste with salt and pepper. • Tagliatelle makes a good accompaniment.

Chicken Drumsticks en Papillote

Especially succulent and highly flavoured

4 x 200g/7oz chicken drumsticks
Salt
1 tbsp sweet paprika
25g/1oz butter
2 shallots
200g/7oz leeks
¼ cauliflower
2 red peppers
125ml/4fl oz chicken stock
2 tbsps medium sherry
2 tbsps snipped chives

Preparation time: 20 minutes
Cooking time: 35 minutes
Nutritional value:
Analysis per serving, approx:
• 1300kJ/310kcal
• 45g protein
• 12g fat
• 9g carbohydrate

Wash the chicken drumsticks and pat dry. Rub with salt and the paprika. Melt the butter, and fry the drumsticks until lightly browned on all sides. • Peel and coarsely chop the shallots. Trim, halve and wash the leeks. Cut into 3cm/1½-inch chunks. Divide the cauliflower into florets, wash and drain. • Halve, seed, wash and chop the peppers. • Transfer the drumsticks to a large sheet of baking foil. Raise the sides of the foil, and add the shallots, leeks, cauliflower, peppers and stock. Seal the foil tightly and pierce the top several times with a needle. • Transfer to a baking sheet, and bake in a preheated oven at 220°C/425°F/gas mark 7 for 35 minutes. • Arrange the chicken drumsticks with the vegetables on a serving dish. Sprinkle over the sherry and chives. • Serve with boiled potatoes.

Chicken Pie

A traditional melt-in-the-mouth pie

1 x 1kg/2¼lb chicken
1l/1¾ pints water
Sea salt and freshly ground black pepper • 250g/8oz wholemeal flour
1 tsp baking powder
Pinch of curry powder
190g/6½oz butter, softened
1 egg, lightly beaten • 1 onion
1 carrot • 100g/4oz mushrooms
1 tbsp finely chopped fresh parsley • 1 tsp torn basil leaves
Pinch of cayenne • 1 egg yolk

Preparation time: 1½ hours
Baking time: 25 minutes
Nutritional value:
Analysis per serving, approx:
• 3900kJ/930kcal • 64g protein
• 58g fat • 43g carbohydrate

Wash the chicken. Place in a large pan and add the water and ½-1 tsp salt. Bring to the boil, lower the heat and simmer for 1 hour. • To make the dough, mix together 200g/7oz of the flour with the baking powder, a pinch of salt, the curry powder and a pinch of pepper. Add 125g/4½oz of the butter and the egg, and knead to form a smooth dough. Loosely wrap the dough and set aside in the refrigerator to rest. • Grease a pie dish with 15g/½oz of the remaining butter, and set aside. • Peel and finely chop the onion. Peel and finely dice the carrot. Wash, pat dry and thinly slice the mushrooms. • Melt the remaining butter, and fry the onion until transparent. Add the carrot and mushrooms, and fry for 5 minutes. • Remove the chicken from the stock. Reserve 250ml/8fl oz of the stock. Skin the chicken and cut the meat from the bones. Cut the meat into 2cm/¾-inch pieces. • Stir the remaining flour into the reserved stock, and pour over the vegetables. Cook, stirring constantly, for a further 5 minutes. Stir in the chicken, parsley, basil and cayenne, and season to taste. • Transfer to the prepared pie dish. • Roll out the dough to fit the dish. Brush the top of the pie with egg yolk. • Bake in a preheated oven at 200°C/ 400°F/gas mark 6 for 25 minutes until golden.

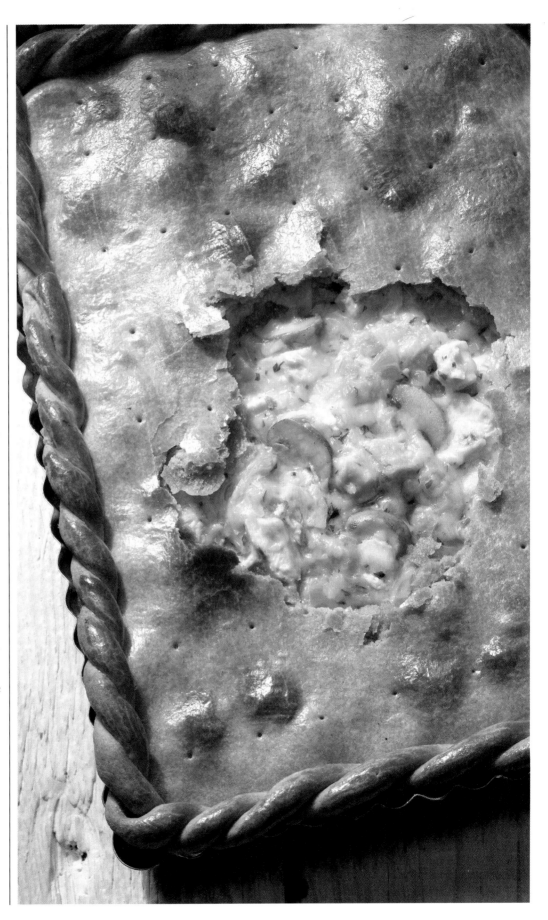

Delicious Dishes from America

Tender poultry with subtly flavoured creamy sauces are particular favourites in the United States

Creamed Chicken
Illustrated left

1 x 1.2kg/2¼ lb chicken
1.5l/2½ pints water
Salt
1 large carrot
2 onions
2 leeks
2 celery stalks
250ml/8fl oz double cream
200ml/7fl oz medium sherry
1-2 tsps curry powder
1 tsp lemon juice
50g/2oz butter
4 slices white bread, cut in half diagonally

Preparation time: 30 minutes
Cooking time: 1½ hours
Nutritional value:

Analysis per serving, approx:
• 3600kJ/860kcal
• 72g protein
• 47g fat
• 44g carbohydrate

Wash the chicken. Bring the water to the boil, add 1 tsp salt and the chicken, and cook over a medium heat. During the first 20 minutes of cooking time, skim frequently. • Peel and chop the carrot. Peel and coarsely chop the onions. Trim, halve, wash and chop the leeks. Trim, wash and chop the celery. • Add the vegetables to the pan, and lower the heat so that the surface of the stock is just rippling. Poach the chicken for a further 1 hour. • Remove the chicken from the pan. Skin the chicken and cut the meat from the bones. Slice into even small pieces. • Place the chicken in a clean pan, and add the cream. Set over a medium heat and allow the cream to reduce slightly. Stir in the sherry, curry powder and lemon juice, and season to taste with salt. If necessary, add a few tablespoons of the stock. • Melt the butter, and fry the bread until brown on both sides. Place 2 triangles of fried bread on each of four individual plates and pour over the creamed chicken. • Serve immediately.

King's Chicken
Illustrated right

200g/7oz mushrooms
600g/1¼ lbs skinless chicken fillets
1 red pepper
Salt and freshly ground white pepper
25g/1oz butter
125ml/4fl oz double cream
2 tbsps flour
125ml/4fl oz chicken stock
Juice of ½ lemon
1 tbsp finely chopped fresh parsley

Preparation time: 35 minutes
Nutritional value:

Analysis per serving, approx:
• 1300kJ/310kcal
• 37g protein
• 14g fat
• 7g carbohydrate

Wash, pat dry and thinly slice the mushrooms. • Cut the chicken into strips about 1cm/½ inch wide. • Halve, seed and wash the pepper. Blanch in lightly salted boiling water for 5 minutes. Drain and finely dice. • Melt the butter, and stir-fry the mushrooms and chicken for 5 minutes. • Beat together the cream, flour and chicken stock. Add the cream mixture and the pepper to the pan. Cook over a low heat for a further 5 minutes, stirring constantly. Add a little hot chicken stock if necessary, to make a light, creamy sauce. • Remove the pan from the heat, stir in the lemon juice and season to taste with salt and pepper. Transfer to a serving dish and sprinkle with the parsley.

Tasty Chicken and Turkey Dishes

Two more tasty ideas – one requiring time for preparation and one very quick

Cherkess Chicken
Illustrated left

1 x 1.2kg/2¹/₂ lb chicken
Salt
2 onions
1 clove
1 bouquet garni
1 bay leaf
1 slice day-old bread, crusts removed
150g/5oz shelled walnuts
2 tsps corn oil
1 tbsp finely chopped fresh parsley
2 tbsps crème fraîche

Preparation time: 40 minutes
Cooking time: 1¹/₂ hours
Nutritional value:
Analysis per serving, approx:
• 3150kJ/750kcal • 71g protein
• 55g fat • 21g carbohydrate

Wash the chicken. Place in a large pan, cover with water and add a pinch of salt. Bring to the boil and poach over a low heat for 30 minutes. Skim frequently. • Peel and quarter 1 onion. Stick 1 quarter with the clove. • Add the onion quarters, bouquet garni and bay leaf to the pan, and cook for a further 1 hour. • Tear the bread into pieces and place in a small bowl. Cover with cold water and set aside to soak. • Grind two-thirds of the nuts and roughly chop the remainder. • Peel and finely chop the remaining onion. Heat the oil, and fry the chopped onion until just beginning to colour. Add the ground walnuts and stir-fry. Remove from the heat. • Squeeze the water from the bread. Mix together the bread, the onion and nut mixture, parsley, chopped nuts and crème fraîche to form a smooth cream, and season to taste with salt. • Remove the chicken from the pan and reserve the stock. Discard the bouquet garni and bay leaf. Skin the chicken and cut the meat from the bones. Cut the meat into even pieces and keep warm. • Rub the stock through a sieve. Return to the pan and reduce over a medium heat. • Mix 250ml/8fl oz of the stock with the nut cream. Stir in the chicken. Transfer to a serving dish, and serve immediately. • Brown rice makes an excellent accompaniment.

Saucy Turkey
Illustrated right

1kg/2¹/₄ lbs turkey escalopes
1 tbsp flour
1 onion
2 tbsps sunflower oil
125ml/4fl oz chicken stock
1 tsp curry powder
150ml/5fl oz crème fraîche
1 tbsp small capers
3 tbsps chopped mixed herbs, e.g. chervil, tarragon and parsley
Salt and freshly ground white pepper

Preparation time: 25 minutes
Nutritional value:
Analysis per serving, approx:
• 1300kJ/310kcal • 39g protein
• 14g fat • 4g carbohydrate

Wash the turkey and pat dry. Cut into thin strips and toss in the flour. • Peel and finely chop the onion. • Heat the oil, and stir-fry the turkey. Add the onion, and fry for 3 minutes. Gradually stir in the stock, and cook over a low heat for a further 5 minutes. • Mix together the curry powder and crème fraîche. Stir the crème fraîche mixture, capers and mixed herbs into the pan, and season to taste with salt and pepper. • Serve immediately with buttered noodles and a mixed salad.

Tasty Family Meals

These recipes prove that chicken is also ideal for substantial meals

Basque Chicken
Illustrated left

1 x 1kg/2¼ lb chicken
800g/1½lbs tomatoes
2 green peppers
2 onions
3 garlic cloves
5 tbsps olive oil
125ml/4fl oz hot chicken stock
Salt and freshly ground black pepper
250g/8oz long-grain rice
1 tbsp mild paprika

Preparation time: 1 hour
Nutritional value:
Analysis per serving, approx:
- 2900kJ/690kcal
- 60g protein
- 28g fat
- 64g carbohydrate

Wash and dry the chicken. Cut into 8 portions. • Skin and quarter the tomatoes. • Halve, seed and wash the peppers and cut into strips. • Peel and finely chop the onions and garlic. • Heat 3 tbsps of the oil, and fry the chicken pieces until golden all over. Add the diced onion and garlic, and stir-fry until transparent. • Add the tomatoes, peppers and stock, and season to taste with salt and pepper. Cover and cook over a low heat for 30 minutes. • Wash the rice under cold running water and drain. Heat the remaining oil, and fry the rice, stirring frequently, for 5 minutes. Add 500ml/16fl oz water and ½ tsp salt. Cover and cook over a low heat for 20 minutes. Stir in the paprika. Transfer the rice to a serving dish and arrange the chicken and vegetables on top.

Chicken with Peanut Sauce
Illustrated right

1 x 1kg/2¼ lb chicken
Sea salt and freshly ground white pepper
15g/½oz butter
100g/4oz carrots
100g/4oz shelled peanuts
2 tbsps wholemeal flour
½ tsp ground turmeric
250ml/8fl oz hot water
2 tbsps finely chopped fresh parsley

Preparation time: 50 minutes
Nutritional value:
Analysis per serving, approx:
- 2300kJ/550kcal
- 59g protein
- 31g fat
- 11g carbohydrate

Wash the chicken and pat dry. Cut into 4 pieces, and rub with salt and pepper. • Melt the butter, and fry the chicken until brown all over. Cover and cook over a low heat for 40 minutes, turning once. • Peel and finely dice the carrots. • Coarsely grind the peanuts. • Sprinkle the ground nuts and the flour over the chicken. Turn the chicken to coat thoroughly. Add the carrots, turmeric and hot water. Cook gently for a further 10 minutes, until the sauce has thickened. • Adjust the seasoning, if necessary, and transfer to a serving dish. Sprinkle with the parsley. • This is delicious served with potato croquettes.

Bolivian Chicken

One of the country's many speciality chicken dishes

1 x 1.5kg/3lb 6oz chicken
2 garlic cloves
3 large onions
4 tbsps olive oil
500ml/16fl oz hot chicken stock or consommé
1 tsp hot paprika
Salt and freshly ground black pepper
400g/14oz tomatoes
1 red pepper
¹/₂ tsp dried oregano
1 tsp caraway seeds
5 tbsps breadcrumbs
2 hard-boiled eggs, shelled and sliced
20 green olives

Preparation time: 40 minutes
Cooking time: 1 hour
Nutritional value:
Analysis per serving, approx:
• 3100kJ/740kcal
• 85g protein
• 39g fat • 21g carbohydrate

Wash the chicken and pat dry. Cut into 8 pieces. • Peel and finely chop the garlic. Peel and thinly slice the onions and push out into rings. • Heat the oil, and fry two-thirds of the onions until transparent. Add the chicken pieces, and fry until browned on all sides. • Add half the stock or consommé and the paprika, and season to taste with salt and pepper. Cover and braise for 40 minutes. • Skin the tomatoes and cut into wedges. Halve, seed, wash and dice the pepper. • Place the tomatoes, pepper, oregano, caraway seeds, garlic, the remaining onion and the remaining stock or consommé in a pan. Bring to the boil, lower the heat, cover and simmer for 20 minutes. • Stir the breadcrumbs into the vegetables. • Arrange the chicken pieces and the vegetables on a serving dish, and garnish with the eggs and olives.

Chicken in Apricot Sauce

A mouthwatering combination

1 large onion
500g/1lb 2oz apricots
1 x 1.2kg/2¹/₂ lb chicken
6 tbsps sunflower oil
2 tbsps flour
About 375ml/15fl oz hot water
2 tsps caster sugar
Salt and freshly ground white pepper

Preparation time: 40 minutes
Cooking time: 30 minutes
Nutritional value:
Analysis per serving, approx:
• 2300kJ/550kcal
• 64g protein
• 25g fat
• 26g carbohydrate

Peel and finely chop the onion. Wash the apricots in lukewarm water. Dry, halve and stone. • Wash the chicken and pat dry. Cut into 8 pieces. • Heat the oil, and fry the chicken over a medium heat until browned on all sides. Remove from the pan. •

Reserve 1 tbsp of the oil and discard the remainder. • Return the pan to a low heat, and stir in the flour. Gradually stir in sufficient hot water to form a thick sauce. • Stir in the onion, and cook over a low heat for 3 minutes, stirring frequently. Stir in the apricots and sugar, and season to taste with salt and pepper. Place the chicken pieces in the sauce. • Cover and braise over a low heat for a further 30 minutes. • This dish may be served with brown rice or mashed potato and any type of salad.

Young Chicken with Herbs and Vegetables

These two recipes for braising chicken result in particularly delicate sauces

Chicken with Aubergines
Illustrated left

3 aubergines

Salt and freshly ground white pepper

1 garlic clove

50g/2oz rindless streaky bacon

300g/10oz ripe tomatoes

1 x 1.2kg/2½lb chicken

6 tbsps olive oil

100ml/3½fl oz dry white wine

½ tsp dried oregano

1 tbsp finely chopped fresh parsley

Preparation time: 1 hour
Nutritional value:

Analysis per serving, approx:
• 2800kJ/680kcal
• 66g protein
• 41g fat
• 11g carbohydrate

Wash and dice the aubergines. Place in a colander, sprinkle with 1 tsp salt and set aside for 30 minutes to drain. • Peel and finely chop the garlic. Dice the bacon. • Skin and chop the tomatoes. • Wash the chicken and pat dry. Cut into 8 pieces. • Heat 3 tbsps of the oil, and fry the chicken, bacon and garlic until the chicken is browned all over. • Add the wine, bring to the boil and allow to reduce slightly. • Add the tomatoes and oregano, and season to taste with salt and pepper. Cover and cook over a low heat for 25 minutes. • Rinse the aubergine in cold water and drain. Heat the remaining oil, and stir-fry the aubergine for 7 minutes. Add to the chicken and tomato mixture. • Transfer to a serving dish and sprinkle over the parsley.

Braised Herb Chicken
Illustrated right

1 x 1.2kg/2½lb chicken, with giblets

40g/1½oz butter

Salt and freshly ground black pepper

Juice of ½ lemon

100ml/3½fl oz dry white wine

3 tbsps chicken stock

5 shallots

3 tbsps finely chopped fresh parsley

1 tbsp torn basil leaves

2 basil sprigs

Preparation time: 45 minutes
Cooking time: 30 minutes
Nutritional value:

Analysis per serving, approx:
• 2100kJ/500kcal
• 63g protein
• 27g fat
• 5g carbohydrate

Wash the chicken and the giblets and pat dry. Cut the chicken into 8 pieces. • Melt the butter, and fry the chicken and giblets until browned all over. Season to taste with salt and pepper. Sprinkle over the lemon juice and add half the wine. Cover and cook over a low heat for 30 minutes, turning several times. • Add the chicken stock. • Peel and finely chop the shallots. • Remove the chicken from the pan and keep warm. • Take out the giblets, reserving the liver. Dice the liver. • Cook the shallots in the cooking juices, but do not brown. • Add the liver and the remaining wine, bring to the boil and allow to reduce. • Return the chicken to the pan to heat through. • Transfer to a serving dish. Sprinkle with the chopped herbs and garnish with the basil sprigs.

Chicken Risotto with Fennel

Chicken and fennel complement each other perfectly

1kg/2¼lbs chicken breast fillets

Salt and freshly ground white pepper

½ tsp dried tarragon

750g/1½lbs fennel

2 onions

1 large garlic clove

6 tbsps olive oil

300g/10oz Arborio or other risotto rice

500ml/16fl oz chicken stock

250ml/8fl oz dry white wine

100g/4oz freshly grated Parmesan cheese

Preparation time: 30 minutes
Cooking time: 20 minutes
Nutritional value:
Analysis per serving, approx:
• 3300kJ/780kcal
• 74g protein
• 21g fat
• 74g carbohydrate

Wash the chicken and pat dry. Slice and rub with salt, pepper and the tarragon. • Reserve some of the feathery fennel leaves. Trim, quarter and wash the fennel bulbs. • Peel and finely chop the onion and garlic. • Heat the oil, and quickly fry the chicken fillets on both sides. Add the fennel, onion and garlic and fry for 3 minutes. • Wash the rice under cold running water and drain. Add to the pan, and stir-fry until transparent. Add the stock and wine, and season to taste with salt. Cover and cook for 20 minutes. • Transfer the risotto to a serving dish, sprinkle over the Parmesan cheese and garnish with the reserved fennel leaves.

Our tip: For an extra special touch, add 50g/2oz toasted pine nuts to the risotto.

Chicken with Olives

A summertime country dish from Italy

1 x 1.2kg/2½lb chicken

2 garlic cloves

1 tsp finely chopped fresh rosemary

2 ripe tomatoes

4 tbsps olive oil

16 black or green olives, stoned

Salt and freshly ground white pepper

3 tbsps chicken stock

2 basil sprigs

Preparation time: 25 minutes
Cooking time: 30 minutes
Nutritional value:
Analysis per serving, approx:
• 2100kJ/500kcal
• 63g protein
• 30g fat
• 4g carbohydrate

Wash the chicken and pat dry. Cut the chicken into 8 pieces. • Peel and finely chop the garlic. Mix together the garlic and rosemary. Skin the tomatoes and cut into wedges. • Heat the oil, and fry the chicken over a medium heat until browned on all sides. Sprinkle over the garlic and rosemary mixture, and fry for a further 5 minutes. Season to taste with salt and pepper. Lower the heat, cover and braise for 15 minutes. • Add the tomatoes, olives and stock, cover, and cook for a further 15 minutes. Add a little more chicken stock, if necessary. • Transfer the chicken and vegetables to a serving dish and garnish with the basil sprigs. • This is especially tasty served with polenta slices or fresh bread.

Chicken Soufflé

The soufflé can also be made in four individual dishes and served as a starter

Chicken Drumsticks with Mushrooms

Serve with the same red wine as that used for the sauce

600g/1¼ lbs chicken breasts
125ml/4fl oz boiling water
1 small bay leaf
½ tsp white peppercorns
2 sprigs parsley
½ tsp dried tarragon
Salt and freshly ground white pepper • 4 shallots
40g/1½oz butter • 2 tbsps flour
6 tbsps double cream
4 tbsps dry white wine
4 eggs
1 tbsp freshly grated Parmesan cheese

Preparation time: 20 minutes
Cooking time: 1 hour
Nutritional value:

Analysis per serving, approx:
• 600kJ/380kcal • 45g protein
• 18g fat • 7.5g carbohydrate

Wash the chicken breasts. Place in a pan, and add the boiling water, bay leaf, peppercorns, parsley and tarragon, and season to taste with salt. Cover and cook for 30 minutes. • Remove the chicken from the pan. Skin and cut the meat from the bones. Cut the chicken into thin strips. Rub the stock through a sieve and reserve. • Peel and finely chop the shallots. Melt 25g/1oz of the butter, and fry the shallots until transparent. Sprinkle over the flour, and cook, stirring constantly, for 2 minutes. Gradually stir in the reserved stock, the cream and wine. Bring to the boil, stirring constantly. Season to taste with salt and pepper, and remove from the heat. • Grease a soufflé dish with the remaining butter. • Separate the eggs. Beat the egg yolks, cheese and chicken into the sauce. • Whisk the egg whites until they form stiff peaks. Fold the egg whites into the chicken mixture. Pour into the soufflé dish and bake in a preheated oven at 200°C/400°F/gas mark 6 for 30 minutes. Serve immediately.

8 chicken drumsticks
4 tbsps flour
1 onion
1 garlic clove
15g/½oz butter
4 tbsps olive oil
1 tbsp tomato purée
100ml/3½fl oz dry red wine
Pinch dried marjoram
Pinch dried thyme
Salt and freshly ground white pepper
1 bunch parsley
350g/11oz mushrooms
Juice ½ lemon
1 tbsp wine vinegar

Preparation time: 40 minutes
Cooking time: 30 minutes
Nutritional value:

Analysis per serving, approx:
• 2200kJ/520kcal • 66g protein
• 22g fat • 13g carbohydrate

Wash the chicken drumsticks and pat dry. Toss in the flour to coat completely. • Peel and chop the onion and garlic. • Melt the butter with 1 tbsp of the oil, and fry the drumsticks, onion and garlic until the chicken is browned on all sides. • Mix together the tomato purée, wine, marjoram and thyme, and season to taste with salt and pepper. Add to the pan, and cook for 30 minutes. • Wash the parsley and shake dry. Reserve a few sprigs for the garnish and chop the remainder. • Finely slice the mushrooms, and sprinkle with the lemon juice. • Heat the remaining oil in another pan, and fry half the chopped parsley and the mushrooms until all the liquid has evaporated. • Add the mushrooms to the chicken drumsticks. Sprinkle with the vinegar and the remaining parsley. • Transfer to a serving dish and garnish with the reserved parsley sprigs.

Szechwan Chicken

A typical stir-fried dish

Chicken with Cheese Sauce

Tasty Gorgonzola gives a wonderfully distinctive flavour to the cream sauce

---

1 x 1kg/2¼ lbs skinless, boneless chicken pieces

3 tbsps light soya sauce

2 tsps cornflour

3 carrots

4 spring onions

1 red chilli

4 tbsps sesame seed oil

Preparation time: 1 hour
Nutritional value:
Analysis per serving, approx:
- 2000kJ/480kcal
- 53g protein
- 22g fat
- 16g carbohydrate

Wash the chicken and pat dry. Cut the meat into thin strips about 4cm/1½ in long. Place in a bowl and sprinkle with the soy sauce and cornflour. Mix well, cover and set aside to marinate for 30 minutes. • Peel the carrots and cut into matchstick strips. Trim and wash the spring onions and cut into matchstick strips. Seed and wash the chilli and cut into very thin rings. • Heat 2 tbsps of the oil in a wok or a large frying pan. Stir-fry the chicken for 5 minutes. Remove from the wok or pan. • Heat the remaining oil in the wok or frying pan. Stir-fry the vegetables for 6 minutes. Return the chicken to the wok or pan, and stir-fry for a further 2 minutes. • This dish may be served with brown rice and soya sauce.

100g/4oz blanched almonds

600g/1¼ lbs chicken breast fillets

Salt and freshly ground white pepper

1 tbsp flour

1 egg, lightly beaten

40g/1½ oz butter

3 tbsps dry white wine

300ml/10fl oz double cream

100g/4oz Gorgonzola cheese

Pinch of grated nutmeg

Pinch of sugar

Preparation time: 30 minutes
Nutritional value:
Analysis per serving, approx:
- 3100kJ/740kcal
- 52g protein
- 54g fat
- 10g carbohydrate

Chop the almonds. • Wash the chicken and pat dry. Rub salt and pepper into both sides. Coat first in the flour, then in beaten egg, and finally the almonds, in that order. Press the coating in place with your fingers. • Melt the butter, and fry the chicken fillets over a medium heat for about 4 minutes on each side. Remove from the pan and keep warm. • Stir the wine and cream into the pan, and bring to the boil, stirring gently. Mash the cheese with a fork, and stir into the pan. Continue stirring until the cheese has melted. Add the nutmeg and sugar, and adjust the seasoning, if necessary. • Divide the Gorgonzola sauce between four individual serving plates, and place the chicken fillets on top. Serve hot. • This dish goes well with tagliatelle and broccoli or a green salad.

Fricassée with Champagne Cream

For a party menu, this fricassée may be served as an entrée

600g/1¼ lbs skinless chicken breast fillets

Salt and freshly ground white pepper

1 tsp finely chopped fresh tarragon

Juice ½ lemon

200g/7oz cooked scampi or king prawns

2 shallots

50g/2oz butter

200ml/7fl oz double cream

1 egg yolk

200ml/7fl oz dry champagne or sparkling dry white wine

Pinch cayenne

Preparation time: 35 minutes
Nutritional value:

Analysis per serving, approx:
- 2100kJ/500kcal
- 45g protein
- 30g fat
- 6g carbohydrate

Rinse the chicken fillets and pat dry. Rub with pepper and sprinkle with the tarragon and the lemon juice. Cover and set aside to marinate for 10 minutes. • Peel, de-vein and wash the scampi. Peel and chop the shallots. • Remove the chicken from the marinade and pat dry. Reserve the marinade. Cut the meat into strips 1cm/¾ inch wide. • Melt the butter, and stir-fry the chicken for 4 minutes until golden brown. Add the shallots, and fry for 1 minute. Add the scampi, and stir-fry for a further 1 minute. • Beat together the cream and egg yolk. Stir into the pan, and heat through, but do not allow to boil. Add the wine and reserved marinade. Reheat but do not boil. • Season to taste with salt and cayenne. • Transfer to a serving dish, and serve with tagliatelle verde or potato croquettes and petits pois tossed in butter.

Succulent Poultry Dishes with Fruit

Breast of duck and guinea fowl make perfect meals for special occasions

Flambéed Breast of Duck
Illustrated right

2 x 300g/10oz boneless duck breasts
350g/11oz plums
15g/½oz butter
2 tbsps brandy
125ml/4fl oz crème fraîche
125ml/4fl oz cream
Pinch ground cinnamon
Pinch cayenne pepper
Salt and freshly ground white pepper

Preparation time: 50 minutes
Nutritional value:
Analysis per serving, approx:
- 1800kJ/430kcal • 36g protein
- 23g fat • 16g carbohydrate

Wash the duck breasts and pat dry. Remove the skin and cut it into strips. • Wash, dry, halve and stone the plums. • Dry-fry the strips of duck skin in a covered pan until the fat runs and they are crisp and brown. Remove from the pan. • Add the duck, and fry, turning frequently, for 3 minutes. Remove from the pan and keep warm. • Melt the butter in a clean pan. Add the plums, and fry until they have absorbed the juice but not disintegrated. • Add the duck and the meat juices to the pan. • Add the brandy, and heat gently. Ignite and allow to burn for 3 seconds, shaking the pan gently. Cover the pan to extinguish the flames. Remove the duck and the plums and keep warm. • Stir the crème fraîche, cream, cinnamon and cayenne into the pan, and season to taste with salt and pepper. • Cut the duck into diagonal slices and arrange on a serving plate. Sprinkle with the crispy skin and spoon the plums next to duck. Hand the sauce separately. • Serve with fried potatoes and a green salad.

Normandy Guinea Fowl
Illustrated left

2 x 800g/1½lb guinea fowl
Salt and freshly ground white pepper • 3 tbsps oil
50g/2oz shelled walnuts
½ tsp dried thyme
250ml/8fl oz cider
200ml/7fl oz crème fraîche
6 tbsps Calvados
2 thin slices rindless streaky bacon
500g/1lb 2oz cooking apples
25g/1oz butter • 1 tsp sugar

Preparation time: 50 minutes
Cooking time: 55 minutes
Nutritional value:
Analysis per serving, approx:
- 4600kJ/1100kcal • 87g protein
- 74g fat • 22g carbohydrate

Wash the guinea fowl and pat dry. Rub with salt and pepper. Heat the oil in a flameproof casserole, and fry the guinea fowl until browned all over. Remove from the casserole. • Reserve 1 tbsp of the oil and cooking juices, and discard the remainder. Add the walnuts and thyme to the casserole, and stir-fry for 1 minute. Add the cider, crème fraîche and Calvados. Place the guinea fowl upside-down in the sauce. Cover the breasts with 1 slice of bacon each. Cover and cook in a preheated oven at 200°C/400°F/ gas mark 6 for 45 minutes. • Peel, quarter, core and slice the apples. Melt the butter, and gently fry the apples for 10 minutes. Sprinkle with the sugar. • Cut the guinea fowl in half and keep warm. • Place the casserole over high heat and boil until the sauce has thickened and reduced slightly. • Transfer the guinea fowl to a serving dish, surround with the apples and hand the sauce separately.

Mediterranean Style Duckling

Use tender young duckling

Duckling with Olives
Illustrated left

1 x 1.6kg/3lb 10oz duckling	
1 onion	
1 garlic clove	
2 tbsps small capers	
3 tbsps olive oil	
3 tbsps finely chopped fresh parsley	
2 tbsps torn fresh basil leaves	
Salt and freshly ground black pepper	
100ml/3fl oz dry white wine	
125ml/4fl oz chicken stock	
2 duck livers	
250g/8oz stoned green olives	

Preparation time: 45 minutes
Cooking time: 1 hour
Nutritional value:
Analysis per serving, approx:
- 4700kJ/1100kcal
- 79g protein • 84g fat
- 5g carbohydrate

Wash the duckling and pat dry. Cut into 8 pieces. • Peel and finely chop the onion and garlic. Finely chop the capers. • Heat the oil in a flameproof casserole, and fry the duckling until browned all over. Reduce the heat, and add the onion, garlic, capers, parsley and basil. Fry for about 10 minutes, stirring frequently. Season to taste with the salt and pepper. • Add the wine, and cook over a low heat, stirring constantly, until the liquid has evaporated. Add the stock, cover, and simmer for about 50 minutes. • Wash the livers, pat dry, trim and finely chop. Stir the olives and livers into the casserole, cover and simmer for a further 10 minutes. • Serve with white bread and tomato salad.

Duckling with Tomatoes
Illustrated right

1 x 1.6kg/3lb 10oz duckling	
2 rosemary sprigs	
6 black peppercorns	
100ml/3½fl oz dry white wine	
100ml/3½fl oz wine vinegar	
1 large onion	
600g/1¼ lbs ripe tomatoes	
4 tbsps olive oil	
Pinch saffron	
Salt and freshly ground black pepper	
5 tbsps chicken stock	

Marinating time: 3 hours
Preparation time: 40 minutes
Cooking time: 1 hour
Nutritional value:
Analysis per serving, approx:
- 4200kJ/1000kcal
- 75g protein
- 77g fat
- 9g carbohydrate

Wash the duckling and pat dry. Cut into 8 pieces, and place in a large shallow dish. • Add the rosemary, peppercorns, wine and vinegar, and set aside to marinate for 3 hours, turning from time to time. • Peel and thinly slice the onion and push out into rings. Skin and roughly chop the tomatoes. • Heat the oil in a flameproof casserole, and fry the onion until golden brown. Add the tomatoes and saffron, and season to taste with salt and pepper. Cover and cook for 15 minutes. • Remove the duckling from the marinade and drain. Add the duckling and stock to the casserole, cover and simmer for 1 hour. Add a little more chicken stock if necessary. • Adjust the seasoning, if necessary • Serve the dish with rice and a green salad.

Wild Duck with Red Wine Sauce

Creamed celery makes this a particularly tasty, complete meal when catering for guests

To serve 6:

1 celery heart • 250g/8oz potatoes • 75g/3oz butter
125ml/4fl oz double cream
Salt and freshly ground black pepper • 2 tsps lemon juice
1 tbsp finely chopped parsley
2 x 1.5kg/3lb 6oz wild ducklings
1 bunch marjoram • 2 shallots
250ml/8fl oz full-bodied red wine

Preparation time: 1 hour
Cooking time: 1 hour
Nutritional value:
Analysis per serving, approx:
• 3200kJ/760kcal • 83g protein
• 38g fat • 17g carbohydrate

Trim, wash and dice the celery. Peel and dice the potatoes. Place in a pan, cover with water and cook for 20 minutes. Drain and transfer to a blender or food processor. Add 25g/1oz of the butter and the cream, and season to taste with salt. Work to form a smooth cream. Transfer to a dish, add the lemon juice and parsley and keep warm. • Place the remaining butter in the freezer to chill. • Meanwhile, wash the ducklings and pat dry. Rub with salt and pepper. • Wash the marjoram, and place half the bunch inside each duckling. Place the ducklings in a roasting tin, and cook in a preheated oven at 220°C/425°F/gas mark 7 for 20 minutes. • Peel and finely chop the shallots. • Remove the ducklings from the roasting tin and carve the breasts into thin slices. Keep warm. Transfer the cooking juices to a small pan. • Return the remaining ducklings to the roasting tin. Lower the oven temperature to 200°C/400°F/gas mark 6, and roast for a further 40 minutes. • Set the pan with cooking juices over a low heat, and add the shallots and wine. Bring to the boil, and cook until reduced by about half. Season. Dice the chilled butter. Stir the butter into the sauce, one piece at a time. • Arrange the duckling breasts on a dish and pour over half the sauce. Cut the remaining meat from the bones, and serve with the breast meat, the remaining sauce and the creamed celery.

Duckling and Turkey Goulash

Two varieties of goulash with quite different flavours – try them and see

Turkey Goulash
Illustrated left

500g/1lb 2oz turkey breast
2 onions
1 cooking apple
400g/14oz celeriac or celery
50g/2oz shelled walnuts
25g/1oz butter
1 tsp mild paprika
1 tsp curry powder
Pinch of ground coriander
250ml/8fl oz hot stock
1 tbsp cornflour
125ml/4fl oz single cream
1 mandarin
Salt

Preparation time: 45 minutes
Nutritional value:
Analysis per serving, approx:
- 1500kJ/360kcal
- 33g protein
- 18g fat
- 17g carbohydrate

Wash the turkey breast and pat dry. Cut into 2cm/³/₄-inch cubes. Peel the onions and cut into wedges. Peel, quarter and core the apple. Peel and dice the celeriac, if using. Trim wash and chop the celery, if using. Coarsely chop the walnuts. • Melt the butter, and fry the turkey until golden brown. Lower the heat, and fry the onions for 2 minutes. Stir in the paprika, curry powder and coriander. Gradually stir in the stock. Add the apple and celeriac or celery. Cover and cook over a low heat for 15 minutes. • Mix together the cornflour and cream to make a paste. Stir the cornflour into the pan and bring to the boil. • Peel the mandarin and separate into segments. Stir into the goulash, and season to taste with the salt. • Transfer the goulash to a serving dish and sprinkle with the nuts.

Duckling Goulash
Illustrated right

To serve 6:

1 x 1.8kg/4lb duckling
Salt and freshly ground black pepper
¹/₂ tsp dried marjoram
2 onions
6 tbsps olive oil
2 tbsps tomato purée
1 tsp mild paprika
250ml/8fl oz dry red wine
125ml/4fl oz chicken stock
300g/10oz mushrooms
16 black olives, stoned
125ml/4fl oz double cream

Preparation time: 40 minutes
Cooking time: 1 hour
Nutritional value:
Analysis per serving, approx:
- 3800kJ/900kcal
- 57g protein
- 67g fat
- 5g carbohydrate

Wash the duckling and pat dry. Cut into 12 portions and rub with salt, pepper and marjoram. Peel and finely chop the onions. • Heat the oil, and fry the duckling quickly until browned on all sides. Remove the duckling pieces from the pan. • Add the onions and tomato purée to the pan, and fry for 5 minutes. Add the paprika, wine and stock, and bring to the boil. • Return the duckling pieces to the pan, cover and braise for 30 minutes. • Wipe the mushrooms and cut any large ones in half. Add the mushrooms and olives to the pan, cover and cook for a further 30 minutes. • Transfer the duckling pieces to a serving dish and keep warm. • Boil the cooking juices, stirring constantly, until reduced by about half. Stir in the cream, and season to taste with salt and pepper. • Pour the sauce over the duckling. Serve with dumplings or potato croquettes.

Braised Turkey Pieces

Rich in protein, light and easy to digest and usually quick to cook

Turkey and Tomatoes
Illustrated left

2 x 600g/1¼ lb turkey drumsticks or thighs	
2 garlic cloves	
1 tsp finely chopped fresh rosemary	
Salt and freshly ground white pepper	
3 tbsps wine vinegar	
5 canned anchovy fillets, drained	
1 x 400g/14oz can tomatoes	
3 tbsps olive oil • 1 tbsp capers	
2 egg yolks	
Juice ½ lemon	
15g/½oz butter	

Marinating time: 2 hours
Preparation time: 30 minutes
Cooking time: 1¼ hours
Nutritional value:
Analysis per serving, approx:
• 2100kcal/500kcal • 70g protein
• 22g fat • 6g carbohydrate

Wash the turkey and pat dry. Peel and finely chop the garlic, and mix with the rosemary. • Rub the turkey with salt, pepper and the garlic and rosemary mixture and place in a shallow dish. Pour over the vinegar, cover and set aside to marinate for 2 hours, turning the turkey several times. • Finely chop the anchovy fillets. Partially drain the tomatoes and coarsely chop. • Remove the turkey from the marinade. Heat the oil, and fry the turkey until golden brown all over. Add the anchovy fillets. Stir in the tomatoes and capers, cover and cook for 1¼ hours. Add a little tomato can juice if necessary. • Remove the turkey from the pan. Skin and cut the meat from the bones. Cut into 3cm/1½-inch cubes. Return the meat to the pan to heat through. • Beat together the egg yolks and lemon juice. Stir the egg yolk mixture and the butter into the pan. Transfer to a serving dish and serve immediately.

Turkey Escalopes with Coriander
Illustrated right

250g/8oz shallots	
1 garlic clove	
4 x 150g/5oz turkey escalopes	
4 tbsps oil	
½ tsp crushed coriander seed	
Salt and freshly ground white pepper	
1 x 400g/14 oz can tomatoes	
1 tsp chicken stock granules	
½ tsp sugar	
¼ tsp cayenne pepper	
1 tbsp coarsely chopped fresh parsley	

Preparation time: 40 minutes
Nutritional value:
Analysis per serving, approx:
• 1100kJ/260kcal • 36g protein
• 10g fat • 9g carbohydrate

Peel the shallots and garlic. Wash the escalopes and pat dry. • Heat the oil, and stir in the coriander. Season the escalopes to taste with salt and pepper. Add to the pan, and fry over a high heat for 1 minute on each side. Remove from the pan. • Add the shallots, and fry until golden brown. Crush the garlic and add to the pan. • Drain the tomatoes, and add the juice to the pan. • Coarsely chop the tomatoes. Add the tomatoes, stock granules, sugar and cayenne pepper to the pan, and cook, stirring, until the mixture has thickened. • Return the escalopes and any meat juices to the pan. Cover and cook over a low heat for 5 minutes. • Sprinkle over the parsley, transfer to four individual plates and serve immediately. • This is delicious served with noodles.

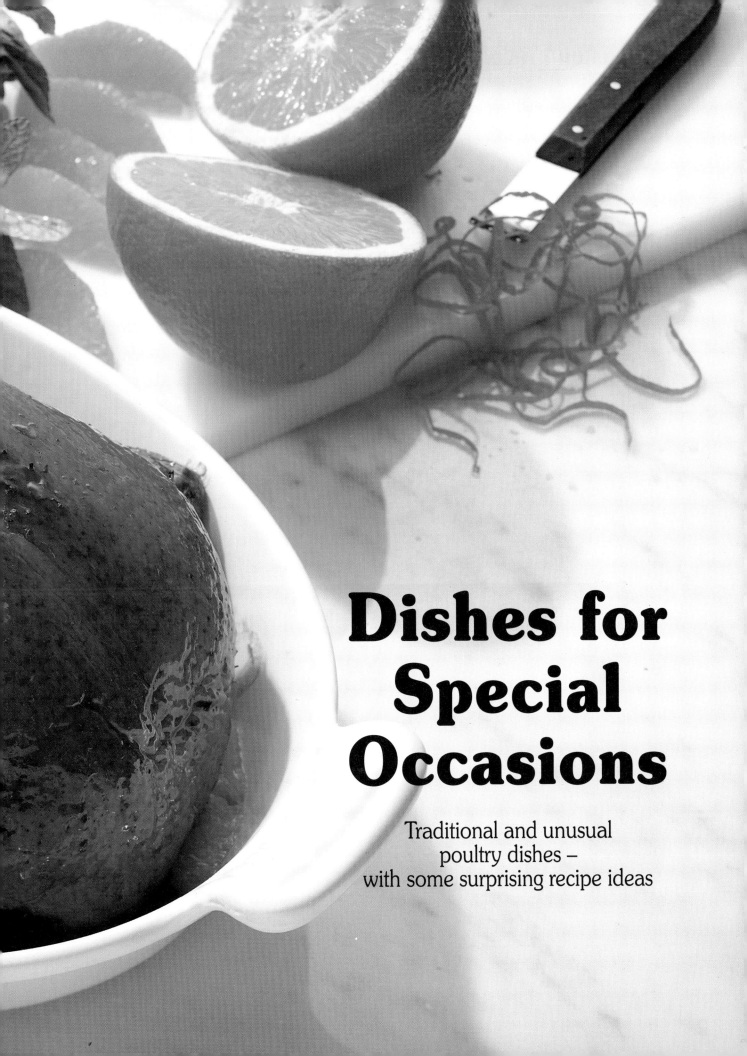

Dishes for Special Occasions

Traditional and unusual
poultry dishes –
with some surprising recipe ideas

Crisp Chicken Pieces

Quick yet popular chicken dishes

Viennese Crisp Fried Chicken
Illustrated left

2 x 700g/1lb 6oz corn-fed chickens
Salt
2 eggs
3 tbsps milk
4 tbsps flour
150g/5oz breadcrumbs
150g/5oz lard
1 bunch parsley
1 lemon

Preparation time: 45 minutes
Nutritional value:
Analysis per serving, approx:
• 2000kJ/475kcal
• 81g protein
• 90g fat
• 31g carbohydrate

Wash the chickens and pat dry. Cut each chicken into 8 pieces, and rub with salt. • Beat together the eggs and milk in a shallow dish. Place the flour and the breadcrumbs on separate plates. Toss the chicken pieces in the flour and shake off any excess. Coat the chicken in the egg and milk mixture and then in the breadcrumbs. Shake off any excess breadcrumbs. • Melt the lard, and fry the chicken pieces, in batches, for 7 minutes or until lightly browned on all sides. Drain on kitchen paper and keep warm. • Wash the parsley and shake dry. Remove the stalks and fry the leaves, in batches, until crisp. • Cut the lemon into wedges. • Arrange the fried chicken on a serving dish garnished with the parsley and the lemon wedges. • Serve with green salad and potato salad.

Roast Chicken Drumsticks
Illustrated right

150g/5oz mushrooms
2 garlic cloves
2 tbsps finely chopped fresh parsley
40g/1¹/₂oz butter
¹/₂ tsp lemon juice
8 x 175g/6oz chicken drumsticks
Salt and freshly ground white pepper
2 tbsps sunflower oil

Preparation time: 20 minutes
Cooking time: 45 minutes
Nutritional value:
Analysis per serving, approx:
• 1900kJ/450kcal
• 65g protein
• 20g fat
• 2g carbohydrate

Trim and wash the mushrooms and pat dry. Peel the garlic cloves. • Work the mushrooms, garlic, parsley, butter and lemon juice in a blender until smooth and creamy. • Rinse the chicken drumsticks and pat dry. Push back the skin at the open end towards the top of the drumstick. Spread the stuffing on the drumstick and pull the skin back over it. Rub with salt and pepper. Sprinkle with the oil and place side by side on a rack in a roasting tin. • Roast in a preheated oven at 250°C/490°F/gas mark 10 for 45 minutes. • This is delicious served with peeled, halved potatoes, which have been covered in a mixture of chopped fresh thyme, salt and a little oil, and roasted in the tin under the chicken. The juices from the chicken add flavour to the potatoes.

Chicken Strudel

This special recipe comes from the Milchmariandl restaurant in Graz

To serve 8:

2 x 1kg/2¼ lb chickens, with giblets
100g/4oz rindless smoked bacon
1 tsp dried thyme
1 tsp dried sage
Salt and freshly ground white pepper
100g/4oz mushrooms
10 large savoy cabbage leaves
2 eggs
2 tbsps finely chopped fresh parsley
125ml/4fl oz double cream
15g/¹/₂oz butter

FOR THE PASTRY:

300g/10oz flour
1 egg
Salt
125ml/4fl oz lukewarm water
1 tbsp sunflower oil
2 tbsps flour
75g/3oz butter

Preparation time: 1½ hours

Baking time: 30 minutes

Nutritional value:

Analysis per serving, approx:

- 3000kJ/710kcal
- 61g protein
- 40g fat
- 30g carbohydrate

Skin the chickens and remove the breasts. Cut the remaining meat from the bones and dice. • Trim the chicken livers. Wash, pat dry and dice. • Cut the bacon into 1cm/¹/₂-inch wide strips. Place the chicken and the bacon on a plate, sprinkle over the thyme and sage, and season to taste with salt and pepper. Set aside in the refrigerator for 30 minutes. • Finely slice the mushrooms. Wash the cabbage leaves, pat dry and remove the stalks. • Make the pastry. Sift the flour onto a clean work surface. Add the egg, ¹/₄ tsp salt and half the water, and knead into a smooth dough. Add a little more water, if necessary. The dough should be smooth and shiny. Shape the dough into a ball, brush with the oil, cover and set aside to rest for 30 minutes. • Put the chicken meat, apart from the breast, through a mincer twice, on its finest setting. • Put the minced meat in a bowl over ice cubes. Stir in the eggs, parsley and cream. Season to taste with salt and pepper. Cover and set aside over the ice for 30 minutes. • Cut the chicken breast into 2cm/³/₄-inch wide strips. Melt the butter, and stir-fry the chicken breast and the livers and over a high heat for 2 minutes. Drain on kitchen paper and set aside. • Roll out the dough on a lightly floured work surface to a large, paper-thin square. Trim off any thick edges. Melt 50g/2oz of the butter and brush over the dough. • Spread half the chicken stuffing over the cabbage leaves. Place the strips of breast meat and the diced liver in the centre. Cover with the remaining stuffing. Place everything on the dough and roll up. • Shape the pastry roll into a horse shoe and lay on the baking sheet. Melt the remaining butter, and brush half of it over the pastry roll. • Bake in a preheated oven at 200°C/400°F/gas mark 6 for 30 minutes. • During the baking time, brush the pastry roll frequently with the remaining melted butter. • Cut the chicken strudel into 16 equal portions, and serve hot with a colourful mixed salad.

Duck Confit

Young goose can be preserved equally successfully using this method

To serve 8:

2 x 2kg/4¹/₂lb ducks

100g/4oz sea salt

1 tsp freshly ground white pepper

1 tsp dried thyme

100g/4oz lard

Preparation time: 40 minutes
Cooling time: 24 hours
Cooking time: 1-2 hours
Nutritional value:
Analysis per serving, approx:
• 5040kJ/1200kcal
• 91g protein
• 98g fat
• 0g carbohydrate

Wash the ducks and pat dry. Cut each duck into 8 pieces. Cut away all visible fat and reserve. • Mix together the salt, pepper and thyme. Rub into the duck pieces and place in deep earthenware dish or chicken brick. Sprinkle with the remaining herb mixture, cover and set aside in the refrigerator for 24 hours. • Melt the duck fat and the lard, and add the duck pieces. Cover and cook over a very low heat for 1-2 hours. Test after 1 hour by piercing the thighs with a darning needle. If the meat juices are clear and pale, the duck is cooked. • Place in layers in a deep earthenware dish or chicken brick. Allow the fat to cool slightly and pour over the duck. It should cover the meat by about 2cm/³/₄ inch to seal. • Set aside in the refrigerator for a further 24 hours, then seal with aluminium foil and a lid or a plate held down with a heavy weight. Store in the refrigerator. • Before it can be eaten the duck must be roasted in a preheated oven at 200°C/400°F/gas mark 6 until crisp and brown. • Serve with red cabbage, sweet chestnuts and potato croquettes. • If only some of the confit is used, the fat must be melted again and poured over the remaining confit. In this way, it will keep for about 10 weeks.

Stuffed Chicken with Brussels Sprouts

A complete and nutritious meal

Barbecued Chicken with Mango Butter

Mango butter makes a tasty accompaniment for chicken

1 x 1.5kg/3lb 6oz chicken
200g/7oz chicken livers
50g/2oz rindless streaky bacon
1 onion • 25g/1oz butter
1 cooking apple
1 tsp finely chopped fresh mint
2 tbsps breadcrumbs
Salt and freshly ground white pepper
1kg/2¼ lbs Brussels sprouts
125ml/4fl oz dry white wine
250ml/8fl oz double cream
Pinch of grated nutmeg

Preparation time: 30 minutes
Cooking time: 1¼ hours
Nutritional value:
Analysis per serving, approx:
• 4200kJ/1000kcal • 100g protein
• 57g fat • 24g carbohydrate

Rinse the chicken and pat dry. Rinse the chicken livers, pat dry and finely dice. Finely dice the bacon. Peel and finely chop the onion. Melt half the butter, and stir-fry the bacon and onion until lightly browned. Add the liver and stir-fry for 1 minute. Remove from the pan, set aside and allow to cool slightly. • Peel, core and grate the apple. Mix together the apple, mint, breadcrumbs and livers, and season to taste with salt and pepper. • Season the inside and outside of the chicken with salt and pepper. Spoon in the liver stuffing and close up with trussing thread. • Melt the remaining butter, and brush over the chicken. Cover with foil and place in a roasting tin. Roast in a preheated oven at 200°C/400°F/ gas mark 6 for 20 minutes. • Trim and wash the Brussels sprouts. • Mix together the wine and cream. Unwrap the chicken, and pour over the wine mixture. Add the Brussels sprouts to the roasting tin. Sprinkle over the grated nutmeg, and season to taste with salt. Replace the foil, and cook for a further 30 minutes. Remove the foil and cook, for a further 25 minutes to brown.

100g/4oz butter
1 tbsp mango chutney
Juice ½ lime
Pinch cayenne
1 x 1.5kg/3lb 6oz chicken
2 tbsps sunflower oil
Salt and freshly ground white pepper

Preparation time: 30 minutes
Cooling time: 1 hour
Cooking time: 30 minutes
Nutritional value:
Analysis per serving, approx:
• 3000kJ/710kcal
• 77g protein
• 50g fat
• 1g carbohydrate

Beat the butter to soften. Mix together the butter, mango chutney, lime juice and cayenne pepper. Form the mango butter into a roll. Wrap in aluminium foil or greaseproof paper, and place in the freezer for 2 hours to set. • Wash the chicken and pat dry.

Cut into 8 pieces, brush with half the oil and season to taste with salt and pepper. • Cook under a preheated hot grill for 30 minutes, turning at least twice and brushing with the remaining oil from time to time. • Cut the chilled mango butter into 8 equal slices and place on the hot chicken pieces. • Serve with curried rice salad, fresh pita bread and an avocado and tomato salad, or sliced, ripe mango.

Our tip: Alternatively the chicken pieces can be cooked on a barbecue.

Sophisticated Spicy Broiling Chicken

Sesame seeds and thyme give a special touch to poultry and game

Sesame Chicken
Illustrated left

1 onion
50g/2oz sesame seeds
25g/1oz butter
2 tbsps sesame oil
2 tsps cracked wheat
Salt and freshly ground white pepper • 1 egg
1 tbsp finely chopped fresh parsley
1 x 1kg/2¼ lb chicken

Preparation time: 30 minutes
Cooking time: 1 hour
Nutritional value:

Analysis per serving, approx:
• 2200kJ/520kcal
• 57g protein
• 33g fat
• 6g carbohydrate

Peel and finely chop the onion. Dry-fry half the sesame seeds. Melt half the butter with half the oil in the pan with the sesame seeds. Add the onion and cracked wheat, and stir-fry until the onion is lightly browned. Remove from the heat. Season to taste with salt and pepper, and allow to cool slightly. Stir in the egg and parsley. • Rinse the chicken and pat dry. Spoon in the stuffing and close with trussing thread. • Season the remaining sesame seeds to taste with salt and pepper, and rub into the chicken. • Melt the remaining butter with the remaining oil. Brush the chicken with half the butter and oil mixture. Place the chicken, breast side down, in a roasting tin and roast in a preheated oven at 220°C/425°F/gas mark 7 for 25 minutes. Turn and roast for a further 25 minutes. • Brush the chicken with the remaining butter and oil mixture and roast for a further 10–15 minutes, basting frequently with the roasting juices. • Turn off the heat and leave the chicken to rest in the hot oven for 10 minutes.

Thyme Chicken
Illustrated right

2 tbsps cracked wheat
50g/2oz leek
15g/½oz butter
1 tbsp finely chopped fresh parsley
2 tsps dried thyme • 1 egg
Sea salt and freshly ground black pepper
1 x 1kg/2¼ lb chicken
15g/½oz butter

Preparation time: 30 minutes
Cooking time: 1 hour
Nutritional value:

Analysis per serving, approx:
• 1700kJ/400kcal
• 54g protein
• 23g fat
• 4g carbohydrate

Place the cracked wheat in a measuring jug and note its volume. Place in a pan with twice the volume of water, bring to the boil and cook for 10 minutes or until all the water has been absorbed. • Trim, wash and finely dice the leek. Melt the butter, and stir-fry the leek until lightly browned. Add the parsley, and stir-fry for 1-2 minutes. Add to the cracked wheat and allow to cool slightly. Stir in half the thyme and the egg, and season to taste with salt and pepper. • Rinse the chicken and pat dry. Spoon in the stuffing and close with trussing thread. • Season the remaining thyme with salt and pepper to taste and rub into the chicken. • Place the chicken, breast side down in a roasting tin. Dot with the butter and roast in a preheated oven at 220°C/425°F/gas mark 7 for 25 minutes. • Turn the chicken over and roast for a further 35 minutes, basting occasionally with the roasting juices during the last 10 minutes. • Turn off the heat and leave in the oven to rest for 10 minutes.

Chicken Masala

Masala is a mixture of a variety of spices

3cm/1-inch piece root ginger	
2 garlic cloves	
$^1/_2$ tsp ground cardamom	
$^1/_2$ tsp cinnamon	
$^1/_2$ tsp cayenne	
2 tbsps lemon juice	
Salt	
2 x 1kg/2$^1/_4$ lb chickens	
150 ml/5fl oz natural yogurt	
100g/4oz blanched almonds	
80g/3$^1/_2$oz seedless raisins	
15g/$^1/_2$oz butter	
250ml/8fl oz water	

Preparation time: 20 minutes
Marinating time: 2 hours
Cooking time: 50 minutes
Nutritional value:
Analysis per serving, approx:
• About 3900kJ/930kcal
• 110g protein
• 51g fat
• 20g carbohydrate

Peel the ginger and garlic and work in a food processor with the cardamom, cinnamon, cayenne, lemon juice and salt to taste, until smooth. • Wash the chickens and pat dry. Cut in half, and place in a roasting tin, cut sides downwards. Brush with the spice paste. • Work the yogurt, almonds and half the raisins in the food processor until smooth, and pour over the chicken. • Melt the butter and drizzle over the chicken. Cover the roasting tin with foil and leave the chicken to marinate at room temperature for 2 hours. • Add 125ml/4fl oz of water to the chicken, cover and roast in a preheated oven at 200°C/400°F/
gas mark 6 for 20 minutes. Lower the temperature to 180°C/350°F/
gas mark 4. Remove the foil and roast the chicken for a further 30 minutes, adding more water if needed. • Stir in the remaining raisins. • Serve the chicken with the sauce and a risotto seasoned with saffron and paprika.

Honey Chicken

A treat for lovers of sweet and spicy flavours

2 x 1kg/2$^1/_4$ lb chickens	
2 tsps sunflower oil	
1 tbsp Dijon mustard	
2 tsps curry powder	
2 tbsps clear honey	
Salt	

Preparation time: 10 minutes
Cooking time: 50 minutes
Nutritional value:
Analysis per serving, approx:
• 2900kJ/690kcal
• 100g protein
• 35g fat
• 4g carbohydrate

Wash the chickens and pat dry. Cut in half. Cut 4 squares of foil large enough to enclose the chicken halves, and brush with the oil. Place the chicken halves on the foil, with the cut surfaces downwards. • Mix together the mustard, curry powder, honey and salt to taste and brush over the chicken. Wrap the foil loosely around the chickens and seal the edges tightly. • Place the chicken halves on a rack above a roasting tin and roast in a preheated oven at 225°C/450°F/gas mark 8 for 30 minutes. Open the foil at the top and roast for a further 20 minutes, until the chicken skin is brown and crisp. • Serve with savoury rice or French fries, accompanied by a crunchy mixed salad.

Our tip: To vary the flavour, you can pour a little white wine over the chicken halves before you seal the foil. Pierce the top of the foil several times with a needle, and cook as above.

Deep-fried Chicken

An especially popular method of cooking crisp chicken pieces

Chicken Wings in Beer Batter
Illustrated left

150g/5oz flour
Pinch of cayenne pepper
Salt
2 eggs
125ml/4fl oz lager
1 tbsp sunflower oil
12 chicken wings
1l/1³/₄ pints vegetable oil
1 lemon
Parsley sprigs

Soaking time: 30 minutes
Preparation time: 1 hour
Nutritional value:
Analysis per serving, approx:
• 2500kJ/600kcal
• 80g protein
• 18g fat
• 28g carbohydrate

Mix together the flour, cayenne pepper and salt to taste.

Separate the eggs. Beat together the egg yolks, lager and oil, and stir into the seasoned flour. Leave the batter to rest for 30 minutes. • Wash the chicken wings and pat dry. • Heat the oil in a deep-fryer to 180°C/350°F or until a cube of stale bread turns golden in 30 seconds. • Whisk the egg whites until stiff, and fold into the beer batter. • Coat the chicken wings in the batter and deep fry, in batches, for 4 minutes or until brown and crisp. • Drain the chicken wings on kitchen paper and keep warm. • Cut the lemon into wedges. • Serve the chicken wings, garnished with the lemon wedges and parsley sprigs, if liked. A potato and radish salad seasoned with fresh herbs makes a tasty accompaniment.

Fried Chicken
Illustrated right

100g/4oz flour
2 eggs
5 tbsps water
Salt and freshly ground white pepper
2 x 800g/1¹/₂ lb chickens
1l/1³/₄ pints vegetable oil

Preparation time: 1¹/₂ hours
Nutritional value:
Analysis per serving, approx:
• 3200kJ/760kcal
• 89g protein
• 43g fat
• 18g carbohydrate

Mix together the flour, eggs, water and salt to taste. Leave to rest, covered, for 20 minutes. • Rinse the chickens and pat dry. Cut each chicken into 8 pieces. • Heat the oil in a deep-fryer to 180°C/350°F or until a cube of stale bread turns golden in 30 seconds. • Coat the chicken pieces in the batter and deep fry, in batches, for 8 minutes or until brown and crisp. Drain the chicken pieces on kitchen paper and keep warm until all the chicken pieces are cooked. Season with salt and pepper to taste. • Serve with peas and sweetcorn or fresh French bread.

Our tip: Chicken breasts or drumsticks can also be cooked in this way.

Chicken Stuffed with Sweetbreads

Just right for a special dinner party

300g/10oz calves' sweetbreads
Salt and freshly ground white pepper
1 x 1.5kg/3lb 6oz chicken
1 tsp dried tarragon
200g/7oz mushrooms •2 shallots
1 garlic clove
100g/4oz beef marrow
1 tbsp finely chopped fresh parsley • 2 tbsps brandy
2 tbsps breadcrumbs • 1 egg
50g/2oz butter
125ml/4fl oz dry white wine
200ml/7fl oz crème fraîche

Soaking time: 5 hours
Preparation time: 1³/₄ hours
Cooking time: 1¹/₄ hours
Nutritional value:
Analysis per serving, approx:
• 5040kJ/1200kcal • 98g protein
• 82g fat • 11g carbohydrate

Wash the sweetbreads. Remove the skin and fibres, then soak the sweatbreads in cold water for 10 minutes to rinse away all remnants of blood. • Wash the chicken and pat dry. Rub the inside with the tarragon and salt, and season the outside with pepper to taste. • Dice the sweetbreads. Finely slice the mushrooms. Peel and finely chop the shallots and garlic. • Mix together the marrow, sweetbreads, mushrooms, shallots, garlic, parsley, brandy, breadcrumbs and egg, and season. Spoon into the chicken and close with trussing thread. • Melt the butter in a roasting tin over a low heat, and fry the chicken until browned all over. Turn the chicken breast side down in the roasting tin and pour over the white wine. • Roast in a preheated oven at 200°C/400°F/ gas mark 6 for 1¹/₄ hours, basting occasionally. • Turn off the heat and leave the chicken to rest, on a grid over a tray, in the warm oven for 10 minutes. • Meanwhile, make the sauce. Pour the roasting juices into a small pan, and stir in the crème fraîche. Bring to the boil and allow to reduce by half. • Remove the trussing thread from the chicken and carve the meat. Hand the sauce separately.

Partridge and Guinea Fowl

Particularly fine game birds with delicious accompaniments

Guinea Fowl with Lentil Purée
Illustrated left

1 onion • 1 garlic clove
50g/2oz rindless bacon
5 tbsps sunflower oil
300g/10oz red lentils
250ml/8fl oz red wine
250ml/8fl oz water
125ml/4fl oz crème fraîche
1 bay leaf
2 x 800g/1½lb guinea fowl
Salt and freshly ground black pepper • 3 juniper berries
4 thin slices of rindless bacon
1 egg • 4 basil sprigs

Preparation time: 15 minutes
Cooking time: 50 minutes
Nutritional value:
Analysis per serving, approx:
• 5880kJ/1400kcal • 178g protein
• 74g fat • 40g carbohydrate

Peel and finely chop the onion and garlic. Dice the bacon. Heat 2 tbsps of the oil, and fry the onions, garlic and bacon for 8 minutes. Add the lentils, 125ml/4fl oz of the wine, the water, crème fraîche and bay leaf, and bring to the boil. Lower the heat, cover and simmer for about 10 minutes. • Wash the guinea fowl and pat dry. Season with salt and pepper to taste. Crush the juniper berries and rub into the guinea fowl. Wrap each guinea fowl in 1 slice of bacon and truss (see page 10). • Heat the remaining oil in a roasting tin over a low heat, and fry the guinea fowl until browned on all sides. Roast in a preheated oven at 220°C/425°F/gas mark 7 for 20 minutes. • Pour over the remaining wine and cook for a further 20 minutes. • Remove the bacon and cook for a further 10 minutes. • Discard the bay leaf and purée the lentils. • Fold in the egg, and season to taste with salt and pepper. Serve the guinea fowl on a layer of lentil purée, garnished with the basil sprigs.

Partridge with Savoy Cabbage
Illustrated right

4 x 600g/1¼lb partridges
Salt and freshly ground black pepper • 50g/2oz butter
200g/7oz small onions • 2 cloves
1kg/2¼lb savoy cabbage
1 tsp dried marjoram • 1 bay leaf
1 carrot
100g/4oz rindless streaky bacon

Preparation time: 1 hour
Cooking time: 30 minutes
Nutritional value:
Analysis per serving, approx:
• 4700kJ/1100kcal • 130g protein
• 66g fat • 16g carbohydrate

Wash the partridges and pat dry. Season to taste with salt and pepper. • Melt half the butter, and fry the partridges until browned all over. Add 3 tbsps of water, cover and simmer for 15 minutes. Reserve the cooking juices. • Peel the onions and dice all but 1. Stud the whole onion with the cloves. Quarter the cabbage, wash and shake dry. Discard the stalk and any tough outer leaves. Roughly shred the leaves. • Melt half the remaining butter, and fry the cabbage until lightly browned. Add 3 tbsps water, the whole onion, cloves, marjoram and bay leaf, cover and cook for 20 minutes. • Halve the partridges. Peel and finely dice the carrot. Finely dice the bacon. Melt the remaining butter, and stir-fry the carrots, bacon and diced onions until lightly browned. • Place half the cabbage in the bottom of a large ovenproof casserole and arrange the partridges on top. Sprinkle over the bacon mixture and cover with the remaining cabbage. Pour over the reserved cooking juices. Cover and cook in a preheated oven at 200°C/400°F/gas mark 6 for 30 minutes. Serve with duchesse potatoes.

Stuffed Guinea Fowl

Fresh guinea fowl is a treat not to be missed

200g/7oz ceps
50g/2oz rindless streaky bacon
15g/¹/₂oz butter • 1 onion
200g/4oz chicken livers
4 tbsps brandy
1 tsp dried tarragon
2 tbsps breadcrumbs
Salt and freshly ground pepper
2 x 800g/1¹/₂lb guinea fowl
4 tbsps vegetable oil
2 tbsps finely chopped fresh mixed herbs • Mixed herb sprig
250ml/8fl oz dry red wine
¹/₂ bay leaf
125ml/4fl oz double cream

Preparation time: 30 minutes
Cooking time: 50 minutes
Nutritional value:
Analysis per serving, approx:
• 4000kJ/950kcal • 98g protein
• 56g fat • 10g carbohydrate

Trim, wash and slice the ceps. • Dice the bacon. Melt the butter, and stir-fry the ceps and bacon until lightly browned. Set aside to cool. • Peel and finely chop the onion. Rinse, and finely chop the chicken livers. Mix together the ceps, bacon, onion, chicken livers, brandy, tarragon and breadcrumbs, and season to taste. • Rinse the guinea fowl and pat dry. Spoon in the stuffing and close up with trussing thread. • Rub the guinea fowl with salt and pepper. • Heat the oil in a roasting tin over a low heat, and fry the guinea fowl until browned all over. Discard the oil. Turn the guinea fowl breast side down. Sprinkle with the mixed herbs and roast in a preheated oven at 200°C/400°F/gas mark 6 for 10 minutes. • Pour over half the wine and add the bay leaf. Return to the oven, and cook for a further 30 minutes. • Remove the guinea fowl from the roasting tin and place on a rack over a tray. Add the remaining wine to the tin. Return the guinea fowl to the oven and roast for a further 10 minutes, basting frequently. • Sieve the roasting juices into a small pan, stir in the cream and allow to reduce by half.

Stuffed Turkey with Chestnut Sauce

A popular, tasty combination for a festive roast turkey

To serve 6:

1 tbsp vegetable oil
1 x 3kg/6¾lb turkey
1 tsp mild paprika
Salt and freshly ground white pepper • 100g/4oz lean veal
500g/1lb 2oz cooking apples
Juice ½ lemon
100g/4oz sausagemeat
200g/7oz chopped hazelnuts
½ tsp cinnamon
250ml/8fl oz hot chicken stock
75g/3oz butter
125ml/4fl oz white wine
150g/5oz canned chestnut purée
200ml/7fl oz double cream
2 tbsps brandy

Preparation time: 45 minutes
Cooking time: 2½ hours
Nutritional value:
Analysis per serving, approx:
• 6300kJ/1500kcal • 110g protein
• 100g fat • 34g carbohydrate

Brush a roasting tin with the oil.
• Wash the turkey and pat dry. Season inside with the paprika and salt and pepper. • Rinse, pat dry and dice the veal. Peel, halve and core the apples. Sprinkle one third of them with half the lemon juice and set aside. Dice the remaining apples and mix with the veal, sausagemeat, hazelnuts, half the cinnamon and the remaining lemon juice. Spoon into the turkey and close up with trussing thread. • Roast the turkey, breast side down, in a preheated oven at 200°C/400°F/gas mark 6 for 1 hour, basting occasionally with the chicken stock. • Turn the turkey over and cook for a further 1½ hours. • Turn off the heat and allow the turkey to rest in the oven for 15 minutes. • Melt the butter in a small pan and add the apple halves. Cook gently until tender but still whole. Rub the turkey roasting juices through a sieve and place in a pan over a medium heat. Stir in the wine, chestnut purée, cream, brandy and the remaining cinnamon, and season to taste with salt and pepper. • Transfer the turkey to a serving dish and remove the trussing thread. Serve with the stewed apple halves, red cabbage and fried potatoes.

Spicy Chicken

Cider and dried fruit give added appeal

Chicken with Dried Fruit
Illustrated left

150g/5oz stoned prunes
150g/5oz dried apricots
1 tbsp raisins • 475ml/15fl oz water • 4 cracker biscuits
1 cooking apple
3 tbsps single cream • 1 egg
2 tbsps brandy
1 x 1.3kg/2lb12oz chicken,with giblets • 2 tsps mild paprika
Salt and freshly ground white pepper • 40g/1¹/₂ oz butter
2 tbsps chopped fresh herbs
200ml/7fl oz crème fraîche

Preparation time: 40 minutes
Cooking time: 1¹/₄ hours
Nutritional value:
Analysis per serving, approx:
• 4200kJ/1000kcal • 74g protein
• 51g fat • 68g carbohydrate

Place the prunes, apricots, raisins and water in a pan and bring to the boil. Drain and reserve the cooking liquid. • Break the cracker biscuits into small pieces. Peel, core and finely dice the apple. Mix together the prunes, apricots, raisins, cracker biscuits, apple, cream, egg and brandy. • Rinse the chicken and pat dry. Rub inside and outside with the paprika. Season the inside with salt and the outside with pepper. • Spoon the fruit stuffing into the chicken and close with trussing thread. Place the chicken in a roasting tin, melt the butter and drizzle over the chicken. Roast in a preheated oven at 200°C/400°F/gas mark 6 for 1¹/₄ hours. • Meanwhile, rinse, pat dry and dice the chicken giblets. Place in a pan and add the reserved fruit liquid and the chopped herbs. Bring to the boil, lower the heat and simmer for 30 minutes. Rub through a sieve and return to the pan. • Transfer the chicken to a serving dish, remove the trussing thread and keep warm. • Stir the roasting juices into the fruit and giblet sauce over a medium heat. Stir in the crème fraîche and beat until well mixed. Hand the sauce separately.

Cider Chicken
Illustrated right

1 x 1.5kg/3lb 6oz chicken
Salt and freshly ground white pepper • 100g/4oz butter
250ml/8fl oz dry cider
750g/1¹/₂lbs carrots
1 tbsp clear honey
4 tbsps finely chopped fresh parsley
125ml/4fl oz double cream
2 tbsps finely chopped fresh tarragon

Preparation time: 30 minutes
Cooking time: 45 minutes
Nutritional value:
Analysis per serving, approx:
• 3800kJ/900kcal • 80g protein
• 56g fat • 27g carbohydrate

Wash the chicken and pat dry. Cut into 8 pieces, and season to taste with salt and pepper. • Melt half the butter in a flameproof casserole, and fry the chicken pieces until browned on all sides. Add the cider, and bring to the boil. Lower the heat, cover and simmer for 45 minutes. • Peel the carrots and cut into 5cm/2-inch chunks. Melt the remaining butter in a small pan. Add the carrots, 4 tbsps water and a pinch of salt. Cover and simmer for 20 minutes until the water has evaporated. Do not allow the carrots to burn. Gently stir in the honey. Sprinkle over 1 tbsp parsley, cover and keep warm. • Arrange the chicken on a serving dish. Keep warm. • Bring the sauce to the boil and allow to reduce by half. Stir in the cream, the remaining parsley and the tarragon, and season. • Serve the chicken with the sauce and the carrots. Parsley potatoes make an excellent accompaniment.

Quail and Chicken with Splendid Stuffings

Both dishes will delight your guests on special occasions

Morel Stuffed Quails
Illustrated left

To serve 6:

25g/1oz dried morels

4 tbsps dry sherry

1 thick slice bread, crust removed

250ml/8fl oz double cream

6 x 200g/7oz quails

Salt and freshly ground white pepper • 250g/8oz minced veal or sausagemeat

2 tbsps finely chopped fresh chervil • Pinch of grated nutmeg

1 shallot • 1 tbsp sunflower oil

50g/1oz butter

Preparation time: 45 minutes
Cooking time: 30 minutes
Nutritional value:

Analysis per serving, approx:
• 2400kJ/570kcal • 46g protein
• 42g fat • 4g carbohydrate

Soak the morels in the sherry. • Dice the bread and sprinkle with 2 tbsps of the cream. Set aside to soak. • Bone the quails, including the wings and drumsticks. • Rub each quail with salt. Remove the morels from the sherry and set aside. Reserve the sherry. Mix together the veal or sausagemeat, chervil, nutmeg, soaked bread and morels, and season to taste. • Spoon equal amounts of stuffing into the quails. Reshape and close with trussing thread. • Peel and finely chop the shallot. Heat the oil and the butter, and fry the quails until browned all over. Transfer to a roasting tin and pour over the oil and butter from the frying pan, the reserved sherry and the remaining cream. Sprinkle over the chopped shallot. Roast in a preheated oven at 220°C/425°F/gas mark 7 for 30 minutes. • Turn off the heat and leave the quails to rest in the warm oven for 5 minutes. • Transfer the quails to a serving dish and remove the trussing thread. Serve with mashed potato.

Sweetcorn Stuffed Chicken
Illustrated right

1 x 1.5kg/3lb 6oz chicken, with giblets • 1 green pepper

25g/1oz butter

100g/4oz minced veal or pork sausagemeat

1 x 200g/7oz can sweetcorn, drained

Salt and freshly ground white pepper • 2 tbsps sunflower oil

1 carrot • 1 onion

1 garlic clove

5 tbsps white wine

5 tbsps chicken stock

125ml/4fl oz crème fraîche

Preparation time: 45 minutes
Cooking time: 1¼ hours
Nutritional value:

Analysis per serving, approx:
• 4100kJ/980kcal • 86g protein
• 53g fat
• 43g carbohydrate

Wash the chicken and pat dry. Wash and pat dry the heart and liver. • Halve, seed, wash and finely dice the pepper. • Melt half the butter, and stir-fry the pepper, heart and liver until browned. Mix with the veal or sausagemeat and sweetcorn, and season to taste with salt and pepper. • Spoon into the chicken and close with trussing thread. Brush with the oil and roast in a preheated oven at 200°C/400°F/gas mark 6 for 1¼ hours. • Peel and grate the carrot. Peel and chop the onion. Peel and chop the garlic. Melt the remaining butter, and stir-fry the carrot, onion and garlic until lightly browned. Add the wine and the stock, bring to the boil and cook for 10 minutes. Rub through a sieve, and mix with the crème fraîche. • Divide the sauce between 4 individual serving plates. Place slices of chicken and stuffing on each of the plates and serve immediately.

Turkey Parcels

Glazed carrots and broccoli with hollandaise sauce make excellent accompaniments to this elegant dish

To serve 6:

6 x 150g/5oz turkey fillets
50g/2oz butter
300g/10oz lean minced beef
125ml/4fl oz double cream
2 eggs
3 tbsps finely chopped mixed herbs
$^1/_2$ tsp mild paprika
Pinch of grated nutmeg
Salt and freshly ground black pepper
6 sheets frozen rough puff pastry dough, thawed
150g/5oz ground hazelnuts
1 egg yolk
2 tbsps milk

Preparation time: 40 minutes
Cooking time: 30 minutes
Nutritional value:
Analysis per serving, approx:
• 3800kJ/900kcal
• 58g protein
• 59g fat
• 37g carbohydrate

Wash the turkey fillets and pat dry. Melt the butter, and fry the turkey fillets until brown all over. Remove from the pan and set aside to cool. • Mix together the minced beef, cream, eggs, herbs, paprika and nutmeg, and season to taste with salt and pepper. • Enclose each fillet completely in the beef mixture. • Place the pastry dough on a clean, lightly-floured work surface. Divide the hazelnuts between the dough sheets, and roll out to 1cm/$^1/_2$ inch thick. • Place 1 fillet on each dough slice. Wrap the dough around the fillets, brush the edges with water and seal carefully. • Rinse a baking sheet with cold water. Transfer the turkey 'parcels' to the prepared baking sheet. • Beat together the egg yolk and milk, and brush over the dough. • Bake in a preheated 200°C/400°F/gas mark 6 oven for 30 minutes.

American Thanksgiving Turkey

Traditionally eaten on Thanksgiving Day in the United States – tasty on other special holidays too

To serve 8:

1 x 4kg/9lb turkey, with giblets
Salt and freshly ground white pepper
1 lemon
2 onions
6 thick slices bread, crusts removed
175g/6oz butter
2 tbsps finely chopped fresh parsley
125ml/4fl oz milk
2 eggs
2 tbsps dried sage
1 tsp chicken stock granules
1 tsp curry powder
750ml/1¼ pints chicken stock
850g/1¾ lbs sweet potatoes
4 tbsps corn oil
4 tbsps sugar
2 tbsps cornflour

Preparation time: 1 hour
Cooking time: 3-3½ hours

Nutritional value:

Analysis per serving, approx:
- 5000kJ/1200kcal
- 110g protein
- 68g fat
- 39g carbohydrate

Wash the turkey and the giblets and pat dry. Rub the inside of the turkey with salt and pepper. • Halve the lemon and rub over the outside of the turkey. • Chop the turkey liver. Peel and chop the onions. Dice the bread. • Melt 50g/2oz of the butter, and stir-fry the onion, liver and parsley until lightly browned. Stir in the bread. Stir in the milk, eggs, sage and stock granules, and season to taste with salt and pepper. • Spoon into the turkey and close with trussing thread. • Place the turkey in a roasting tin. Melt half the remaining butter, and stir in the curry powder. Brush the flavoured butter all over the turkey. Brush a large piece of aluminium foil with any remaining

curry butter, and cover the turkey with it. • Roast the turkey in a preheated oven at 175°C/350°F/gas mark 4 for 1½ hours. Heat the stock. Add the remaining giblets to the roasting tin with the turkey. Gradually pour over the hot stock. Cook for a further 1½ hours, basting frequently with the roasting juices. • At the same time, peel the sweet potatoes, cutting any large ones in half. Heat the oil and the remaining butter and coat the sweet potatoes. Roast in the oven for 1 hour. Remove and sprinkle with the sugar. Increase the oven temperature to 220°C/425°F/gas mark 7, and return the sweet potatoes for a further 30 minutes. • Test the turkey to see if it is cooked by piercing the thickest part of the thigh with a darning needle. If the juices run clear, the turkey is cooked. If it is not, return it to the oven for a further 30 minutes or until it is cooked. Remove the turkey from the oven,

cover with foil and set aside to rest. • Carve the turkey, arrange on a serving plate with the sweet potatoes and keep warm. • Skim the fat from the turkey roasting juices. Finely chop the heart and slice the meat from the neck. Discard any bones and the rest of the giblets. • Dilute the pan juices with the remaining stock. Pour into a small pan and heat until nearly boiling. Add the chopped meat. Mix the cornflour with 2 tbsps cold water to form a smooth paste. Stir into the stock. Bring to the boil, stirring constantly. Lower the heat and simmer for 1-2 minutes, stirring constantly, until thickened. Season to taste with salt and pepper. • Serve the turkey with cranberry sauce and peas tossed in butter and hand the sauce separately.

Pheasant for Festive Roasts

Courgettes and potato croquettes make particularly good accompaniments

Pheasant with Bacon Sauce
Illustrated right

1 x 1.2kg/2¹/₂lb pheasant, with giblets
Salt and freshly ground black pepper
8 thin slices rindless bacon
50g/2oz butter
1 carrot
150g/5oz leeks
2 tbsps sunflower oil
2 tbsps finely chopped fresh parsley
2 crushed juniper berries
5 peppercorns
500ml/16fl oz water
125ml/4fl oz grape juice
3 tbsps dry sherry
125ml/4fl oz crème fraîche

Preparation time: 40 minutes
Cooking time: 40 minutes
Nutritional value:
Analysis per serving, approx:
- 4200kJ/1000kcal • 65g protein
- 78g fat • 12g carbohydrate

Wash the pheasant and pat dry. Cut off the wings. Rub the inside of the pheasant with salt and pepper. • Wrap the breast in half the bacon slices. • Melt the butter in a roasting tin, and fry the pheasant until browned all over. • Roast the pheasant, breast side down, in a preheated oven at 220°C/425°F/gas mark 7 for 30 minutes. • Remove the bacon and discard. Turn the pheasant over and roast for a further 10 minutes to brown the breast. • Dice the remaining bacon. Peel and finely chop the carrot. Trim, halve, wash, and thinly slice the leek. • Heat the oil, and fry the bacon. Add the pheasant wings and giblets, and fry until lightly browned. Add the carrot, leek, parsley, juniper berries, peppercorns and water, and season to taste with salt and pepper. Bring to the boil. Lower the heat, cover and simmer for 20 minutes. • Discard the wings. Rub the sauce through a sieve. • Transfer the pheasant to a serving dish and keep warm. • Place the sauce and roasting juices in a small pan over a medium heat. Stir in the grape juice and the sherry, bring to the boil and allow to reduce to 250ml/8fl oz. Stir in the crème fraîche.

Stuffed Pheasant
Illustrated left

1 x 1.2kg/2¹/₂lb pheasant
100g/4oz smoked ham
175g/6oz rindless streaky bacon
Salt and freshly ground black pepper
2 tsps finely chopped fresh sage
¹/₂ tsp grated lemon peel
4 tbsps olive oil
125ml/4fl oz dry white wine

Preparation time: 20 minutes
Cooking time: 40 minutes
Nutritional value:
Analysis per serving, approx:
- 700kJ/880kcal
- 68g protein
- 65g fat
- 10g carbohydrate

Wash the pheasant and pat dry. Finely dice the ham and half the bacon. Mix together the sage, lemon peel, diced ham and bacon, and season to taste with salt and pepper. • Season the inside of the pheasant with salt, spoon in the stuffing and close with trussing thread. • Heat the oil in a roasting tin, and fry the pheasant until browned all over. Turn breast side down and wrap in the remaining bacon slices. Add the wine. • Roast in a preheated oven at 220°C/425°F/gas mark 7 for 30 minutes, basting frequently with the roasting juices. Remove the bacon slices, turn over and roast for a further 10 minutes to brown the breast.

Turkey Breast with Yogurt Sauce

Turkey breast goes well with a spicy sauce

1 x 1kg/2¼ lb skinless turkey breast fillet

2 garlic cloves

Salt and freshly ground black pepper

6 tbsps sunflower oil

1 yellow pepper

1 red pepper

200g/7oz leeks

500g/1lb 2oz cucumber

125ml/4fl oz hot chicken stock

250ml/8fl oz natural yogurt

2 tbsps finely chopped fresh chervil

Preparation time: 40 minutes
Cooking time: 45 minutes
Nutritional value:

Analysis per serving, approx:
- 1800kJ/430kcal
- 54g protein
- 17g fat
- 13g carbohydrate

Rinse the turkey breast and pat dry. • Peel the garlic, and crush with salt and pepper to taste. Mix with 1 tbsp of oil. Brush over the meat and set aside in the refrigerator to marinate for 30 minutes. • Halve, seed, wash and chop the peppers. Trim and wash the leeks. Cut into 1cm/½-inch chunks. Peel and finely dice the cucumber. • Heat the remaining oil. Place the turkey breast in a roasting tin and drizzle over the hot oil. Roast in a preheated oven at 200°C/400°F/gas mark 6 for 30 minutes. • Arrange the peppers and the leeks around the turkey breast. Pour over the hot chicken stock, and roast the turkey for a further 10 minutes. Add the cucumber, and roast the turkey for a further 5 minutes. • Cut the turkey into slices. Transfer the turkey and the vegetables to a serving dish and keep warm. • Set the roasting tin over a low heat, and stir in the yogurt. Heat through. Pour over the turkey and sprinkle with the chervil. Serve immediately.

Spicy Turkey Escalopes

Mediterranean vegetables and fresh herbs provide the flavour

Turkey Escalopes on a Bed of Courgettes
Illustrated left

1kg/2¹/₄ lbs courgettes	
4 shallots	
4 tbsps sunflower oil	
125ml/4fl oz hot chicken stock	
1 tsp mild paprika	
Salt and white pepper	
4 x 150g/5oz turkey escalopes	
Juice ¹/₂ lemon	
2 tbsps finely chopped fresh parsley	
2 tsps soya sauce	

Preparation time: 40 minutes
Nutritional value:

Analysis per serving, approx:
• 1800kJ/430kcal • 35g protein
• 25g fat • 18g carbohydrate

Trim and wash the courgettes and cut into strips. • Peel the shallots, halve lengthways and slice. Heat 2 tbsps oil, and fry the shallots until transparent. Add the courgettes, cover and fry over a low heat for 5 minutes. Add the chicken stock and paprika, and season to taste with pepper. Partly cover and simmer for a further 10 minutes. Remove the lid, and continue cooking until almost all the liquid has evaporated. • Beat the escalopes until thin, and season with pepper to taste. Divide the remaining oil between 2 large frying pans. Heat the oil, and fry the escalopes for 2-3 minutes on each side until well browned. • Season the vegetables to taste with salt, and sprinkle over the lemon juice and parsley. • Arrange the escalopes and vegetables on a serving dish. Sprinkle over the soya sauce and serve with boiled potatoes.

Turkey Escalopes with Sage
Illustrated right

1 turkey liver	
50g/2oz ham	
3 canned anchovy fillets	
1 tbsp capers	
1 garlic clove	
Grated peel 1 lemon	
8 x 75g/3oz turkey escalopes	
4 tbsps olive oil	
1 tsp finely chopped fresh sage	
Juice ¹/₂ lemon	
Salt and freshly ground white pepper	

Preparation time: 35 minutes
Nutritional value:

Analysis per serving, approx:
• 1600kJ/380kcal • 55g protein
• 17g fat • 2g carbohydrate

Wash the liver and pat dry. Finely dice. Finely chop the ham, anchovy fillets and capers. Peel and crush the garlic. Mix together the turkey liver, ham, anchovy fillets, capers, garlic and lemon peel. • Wash the turkey escalopes and pat dry. • Divide the oil between 2 large frying pans and heat. Divide the liver mixture between the 2 pans and stir-fry until lightly browned. Place 4 escalopes in each pan, on top of the liver mixture. Sprinkle over the sage and lemon juice, and season to taste with salt and pepper. Fry for 2-3 minutes on each side until cooked through. Place the liver mixture on a large serving dish and lay the escalopes on top. • Rice and peas make a tasty accompaniment.

Crisp Roast Duck

Plump, young duckling is best for roasting

Roast Wild Duckling

Illustrated right

200g/7oz ceps

100g/4oz rindless streaky bacon

1 onion • 15g/¹/₂oz butter

1 tsp dried tarragon • 4 tbsps brandy • Salt and freshly ground white pepper

300g/10oz lean minced beef

4 tbsps breadcrumbs

1 x 1.5kg/3lb 6oz wild duckling

4 tbsps sunflower oil • 2 apples

125ml/4fl oz hot chicken stock

125ml/4fl oz dry white wine

Preparation time: 40 minutes
Cooking time: 1¹/₂ hours
Nutritional value:

Analysis per serving, approx:
• 5460kJ/1300kcal • 89g protein
• 90g fat • 17g carbohydrate

Trim, wash, pat dry and thinly slice the ceps. Slice half the bacon into matchstick strips and dice the remainder. Peel and finely chop the onion. • Melt the butter, and fry the diced bacon until the fat runs. Add the onion, and stir-fry until transparent. Add the mushrooms, and stir-fry until tender. Add the tarragon and brandy, and season. Mix the fried stuffing with the minced beef and the breadcrumbs. • Rinse the duckling and pat dry. Spoon in the stuffing and close with trussing thread. • Heat the oil in a roasting tin over a medium heat, and fry the duckling until browned all over. Roast in a preheated oven at 200°C/400°F/gas mark 6 for 30 minutes. • Peel and core the apples and cut into wedges. Add the apples and the chicken stock to the roasting tin, and cook for a further 30 minutes. Pour over the wine and cook for a further 30 minutes, basting frequently with the roasting juices. • Pour off the roasting juices, season, and hand the sauce separately.

Duckling with Almonds

Illustrated left

1 x 1.8kg/4lb duckling with giblets • 1 garlic clove

500ml/16fl oz water

250ml/8fl oz sherry

Salt and freshly ground pepper

1 onion • 125ml/4fl oz oil

150g/5oz blanched almonds

1 tbsp cornflour • Pinch sugar

4 tbsps soya sauce

Preparation time: 30 minutes
Cooking time: 1¹/₂ hours
Nutritional value:

Analysis per serving, approx:
• 5800kJ/1400kcal • 89g protein
• 110g fat • 14g carbohydrate

Rinse the duckling and the giblets and pat dry. Peel and quarter the garlic. Cut the wings from the duckling. Place the water, sherry, garlic, giblets and wings in a large pan. Season, and bring to the boil. • Quarter the duckling, and place in the boiling stock. Lower the heat, and simmer for 1 hour. • Remove the duckling quarters and set aside. • Strain the stock and skim off the fat. Return to the pan, bring to the boil and allow to reduce to 475ml/15fl oz. • Remove the bones from the duckling quarters, but keep the meat whole. • Peel and slice the onion into rings. Heat the oil, and fry the almonds and onion until lightly browned. Remove from the pan and set aside. Fry the duckling quarters, skin side down, until browned. Transfer to a serving dish, sprinkle over the almonds and onion rings, and keep warm. • Mix together the cornflour and 2 tbsps cold water to make a smooth paste. Heat the stock until nearly boiling and stir in the cornflour mixture until thickened. Add the sugar and soya sauce, and season to taste with pepper. • Serve the duckling immediately, and hand the sauce separately.

Duck à l'Orange

A classic way to cook duck

To serve 6:

1 x 1.6kg/3lb10oz duck
1 carrot
1 onion
3 oranges
1 lemon
Salt and freshly ground white pepper
2 tbsps sunflower oil
1 tbsp very finely chopped fresh parsley
475ml/15fl oz hot chicken stock
75g/3oz sugar
1 tsp black peppercorns
4 tbsps white wine vinegar
4 tbsps Cointreau
2 tbsps cornflour
2 tbsps orange marmalade

Preparation time: 45 minutes
Cooking time: about 1¼ hours
Nutritional value:

Analysis per serving, approx:
• 3200kJ/760kcal • 49g protein
• 49g fat • 28g carbohydrate

Rinse the duck and pat dry. • Peel and finely dice the carrot. Peel and finely chop the onion. • Peel 1 orange and remove the white pith. Divide into segments. Using a sharp knife, pare the peel from 1 of the remaining oranges and the lemon. Shred very finely. Squeeze the juice from the remaining oranges and the lemon. Mix the juices and set aside. • Rub the inside of the duck with salt and pepper and close with trussing thread. • Place the oil in a roasting tin and heat in the oven at 200°C/400°F/gas mark 6. Place the duck, breast side down, in the hot oil and roast for 15 minutes. • Sprinkle the carrot, onion and parsley around the duck. Turn the duck on its side and roast for a further 15 minutes. Turn it onto the other side and roast for a further 15 minutes. Turn the duck onto its back, pour over the hot chicken stock, add the orange segments and roast for a further 25 minutes or until it is

done. • Meanwhile, melt the sugar in a small pan over a low heat until golden. Stir in the peppercorns, orange peel, lemon peel and the mixed fruit juices. Bring to the boil, lower the heat and simmer for 30 minutes. • Remove the duck from the roasting tin and cut into portions. Transfer the duck and the orange segments to a serving dish and keep warm. • Skim the fat from the roasting juices. Stir the juices and the wine vinegar into the fruit juice mixture and bring to the boil. Lower the heat and simmer for 1 minute. Remove the sauce from the heat and stir in the Cointreau. • Mix the cornflour with 2 tbsps cold water to make a smooth paste. Stir into the sauce and bring to the boil, stirring constantly. Stir in the marmalade, and season to taste with salt. • Spoon a little sauce over the duck, and hand the remainder separately. This is delicious served with almond croquettes and French beans.

Our tip: To make the sauce as low in fat as possible, allow the roasting juices to cool completely, then remove the congealed fat from the surface. Reheat the roasting juices before adding the fruit juice and vinegar. If you are doing this, wrap the duck in a double layer of foil and keep warm in the oven at its lowest setting.

estive Roast Goose

An exquisite gourmet meal, with spicy sauce or fruit stuffing

Goose with Cranberry Sauce
Illustrated left

To serve 6:

1 x 3kg/6³/₄ lb goose, with giblets
Salt and freshly ground black pepper
250ml/ 8fl oz boiling water
250ml/8fl oz cranberry sauce
125ml/4fl oz dry red wine
¹/₄ tsp ground cloves
¹/₄ tsp grated nutmeg
1 tsp sugar

Preparation time: 20 minutes
Cooking time: 2¹/₂ hours
Nutritional value:
Analysis per serving, approx:
• 5920kJ/1410kcal • 64g protein
• 129g fat • 5g carbohydrate

Rinse the goose and giblets and pat dry. Rub with salt and pepper. • Finely chop the giblets. • Close the goose with trussing thread and place, breast side down, in a roasting tin. Add the giblets and the boiling water. Roast the goose in a preheated oven at 180°C/350°F/gas mark 4 for 1 hour. Turn the goose over and pierce the skin of the drumsticks several times so that the fat can run out. • Roast the goose for a further 1¹/₂ hours, adding more hot water if necessary. • Skim the fat from the roasting juices several times during cooking, and brush the goose several times with cold, lightly salted water. • Test the goose by piercing the thickest part of the thigh with a darning needle. When the juices run clear, the goose is ready. • Remove the goose from the roasting tin and keep warm. • Mix together the cranberry sauce, wine, ground cloves, nutmeg and sugar. Dilute the roasting juices with a little boiling water, strain and stir in the cranberry sauce mixture. Bring to the boil, stirring constantly, and season to taste.

Goose Stuffed with Dried Fruit
Illustrated right

To serve 8:

100g/4oz sultanas
200g/7oz stoned prunes
200g/7oz dried figs • 2 oranges
1 x 4kg/9lb goose, with giblets
Salt and freshly ground pepper
250ml/8fl oz boiling water

Preparation time: 40 minutes
Cooking time: 3¹/₂ hours
Nutritional value:
Analysis per serving, approx:
• 6550kJ/1560kcal • 65g protein
• 129g fat • 40g carbohydrate

Place the sultanas and prunes in a bowl, cover with hot water and leave to soak for 15 minutes. Drain. • Wash the figs in warm water and dice. Finely pare the peel from the oranges and shred. Reserve the flesh. • Wash the goose liver and heart and pat dry. Finely dice, and mix with the dried fruit and the orange peel. • Rinse the goose and pat dry. Rub the inside with salt and pepper. Spoon in the fruit stuffing and close with trussing thread. • Place on a rack over a roasting tin. Pour the boiling water into the tin. Roast in a preheated oven at 180°C/350°F/gas mark 4 for 1 hour. • Turn the goose over and pierce the skin of the drumsticks several times with a darning needle so that the fat can run out. Roast for a further 2 hours, brushing frequently with cold, lightly salted water. • Place the left-over stuffing in an ovenproof dish and bake in the oven, with the goose, for 30 minutes. • Transfer the goose to a serving dish and keep warm. • Remove any remaining pith from the reserved oranges. Arrange orange segments around the goose. • Dilute roasting juices with hot water and strain to make a thin gravy. Hand separately.

Traditional Christmas Goose

Dumplings and red cabbage are ideal accompaniments for roast goose with a chestnut stuffing

To serve 8:

750g/1½ lbs sweet chestnuts
500ml/16fl oz chicken stock
1 x 5kg/11lb 4oz goose
Salt and freshly ground pepper
500g/1lb 2oz cooking apples
100g/4oz raisins • ½ tsp dried sage
250ml/8fl oz boiling water
2 tsp cornflour • ½ tsp sugar

Preparation time: 1 hour
Cooking time: 4 hours
Nutritional value:
Analysis per serving, approx:
• 6870kJ/1635kcal • 76g protein
• 124g fat • 58g carbohydrate

Cut a cross in the chestnuts and roast in a preheated oven at 180°C/350°F/gas mark 4 until the skins burst. Cool slightly then peel. • Bring the chicken stock to the boil. Add the chestnuts and boil for 10 minutes. Drain and allow to cool. • Rinse the goose and pat dry. Rub with salt and pepper. • Peel, core and slice the apples. Wash the raisins and pat dry and mix with the chestnuts, apples and sage. Spoon the stuffing into the goose and truss. • Place the goose, breast side down on a rack over a roasting tin. Pour the boiling water into the tin, and roast the goose in a preheated oven at 180°C/350°F/gas mark 4 for 1 hour. • Turn the goose over and pierce the skin of the drumsticks so that the fat can run out. Roast the goose for a further 2½ hours. • Brush with cold, salted water to crisp the skin and return to the oven for a further 30 minutes. • Transfer the goose to a serving dish, and keep warm. • Skim the fat from the roasting juices. Dilute the roasting juices with a little hot water and strain. Make up to 500ml/16fl oz with water. Set over a medium heat and bring to the boil. Mix together the cornflour and 2 tbsps cold water to make a smooth paste. Stir the paste into to the roasting juices. Cook, stirring constantly, until thickened. Stir in the sugar, and season to taste with salt and pepper. • Serve the goose and hand the sauce separately.

Cold Poultry Cuisine

Pies, delicious pastries
and special salads
for party buffets

Turkey Mousse with Two Sauces

A luxurious summer treat

To serve 6:
400g/14oz turkey or chicken livers
400g/14oz turkey or chicken fillet
50g/2oz butter
2 shallots
1/4 tsp ground allspice
1/4 tsp dried marjoram
1/4 tsp dried thyme
1/4 tsp sugar
Salt and freshly ground black pepper
3 tbsps port
5 egg whites
15g/1/2 oz powdered gelatine
250ml/8fl oz double cream
125ml/4fl oz chicken stock

FOR THE SAUCES:
4 cooking apples
1 tbsp sugar
1/4 tsp cinnamon
125ml/4fl oz apple juice
200g/7oz blackberries or elderberries

Juice 1 lemon
1 tsp maple syrup
Pinch cayenne
Salt
1 slice orange
Marjoram sprigs

Preparation time: 1 1/2 hours
Cooling time: 25 hours
Nutritional values:
Analysis per serving approx:
• 1900kJ/450kcal
• 34g protein
• 24g fat
• 20g carbohydrate

Trim and rinse the turkey or chicken livers. Pat dry and slice. Wash, dry and finely dice the turkey or chicken fillet. • Melt half the butter, and stir-fry the liver over a low heat for about 7 minutes. Remove from the pan with a slotted spoon, and set aside. • Peel and finely chop the shallots. Fry in the same pan until transparent. Remove and set aside with the liver. • Melt the remaining butter in the same pan, and stir-fry the fillet over a medium heat for 10 minutes. • Remove from the pan and allow to cool. Put through a mincer twice on its finest setting. • Finely chop the liver. Mix together the liver, minced fillet, allspice, marjoram, thyme and sugar, and season to taste with salt and pepper. Stir in the port. Set aside in the refrigerator to chill. • Beat the egg whites with a pinch of salt until stiff. • Sprinkle the gelatine onto a small bowl of hot water. Set aside for 5 minutes to soften. Beat the cream until stiff. • Heat the chicken stock. Stir the gelatine, and add to the chicken stock in a continuous stream, stirring constantly. Leave the chicken stock to cool, stirring frequently. • Remove the minced fillet mixture from the refrigerator. Mix with the stiffly beaten egg whites and the cream. Stir in the chicken stock. Pour into a large earthenware dish, smooth the surface with a spatula and cover with a double layer of foil. Set aside in the refrigerator to set for 24 hours. • Make the apple sauce. Peel, quarter, core and dice the apples. Place in a small pan with the cinnamon, sugar and apple juice and bring to the boil. Lower the heat and simmer, covered, for 10 minutes. Purée in a blender or rub through a sieve and set aside to cool. • Make the blackberry or elderberry sauce. Top and tail the berries, reserving a few for the garnish. Purée the berries in a blender or rub through a sieve. Stir in the lemon juice, maple syrup and cayenne, and season to taste with salt. Quarter the orange slice. Garnish the mousse with the orange slice, marjoram and the reserved berries. • Hand the sauces separately. Serve with fresh, crusty bread.

Russian Chicken Pie

A traditional starter for festive menus

Makes 1 x 30cm/12-inch pie
To serve 8:
800g/1½ lbs cooked skinless, boneless chicken
60g/2½ oz butter
200g/7oz long-grain brown rice
Salt and freshly ground black pepper
500g/1lb 2oz mushrooms
3 hard-boiled eggs, shelled
125ml/4fl oz double cream
1 tbsp finely chopped fresh dill
1 tbsp finely chopped fresh parsley
FOR THE PASTRY:
250g/8oz flour
3 tbsps water
Salt
125g/5oz butter
1 egg yolk
1 tbsp cream

Preparation time: 1 hour
Resting time: 2 hours
Cooking time: 3 minutes

Nutritional value:
Analysis per serving, approx:
- 2250kJ/535kcal
- 46g protein
- 27g fat
- 43g carbohydrate

First make the pastry dough. Dice the butter. Sift the flour and a pinch of salt onto a clean work surface, and make a hollow in the centre. Pour in the water and distribute the butter around the edge. Mix together with your hands, pulling the ingredients from the outside into the centre, and knead into a smooth dough. Shape the dough into a roll. Wrap in greaseproof paper and set aside to rest in the refrigerator for 2 hours. • Make the filling. Dice the chicken. • Melt 25g/1oz of the butter, and fry the rice, stirring constantly, until translucent. Pour in sufficient water to cover. Add a pinch of salt, bring to the boil, stir once and lower the heat. Cover, and simmer for 20-30 minutes until the rice is tender and all the water has been absorbed. • Thinly slice the mushrooms. Melt 25g/1oz of the remaining butter, and stir-fry the mushrooms until all the liquid has evaporated. Remove from the pan, and season to taste with salt and pepper. Set aside. • Finely chop the eggs. • Mix together the rice, chicken, mushrooms and diced egg and stir in the cream. • Stir in the dill and parsley, and season to taste with salt and pepper. • Grease a 30cm/12-inch springform cake tin with the remaining butter. • Divide the dough into 2 pieces, 1 slightly larger than the other. Roll out the larger piece of dough on a lightly-floured work surface, until it is a little larger than the cake tin. Line the cake tin with the dough, easing it carefully with your fingers so that it comes up around the sides of the tin and forms a lip around the edge. Prick the base with a fork. • Spoon in the filling and smooth the surface. • Roll out the other piece of dough and dampen the edges with water. Cover the pie with the second piece of dough, and press the edges together firmly to seal. Trim the dough to fit and prick the top with a fork. Roll out the trimmings and make a decorative edging or shapes, if liked. • Beat the egg yolk and the cream and brush the pie with the mixture. Apply any decorations and brush again with the egg yolk and cream. • Bake in a preheated oven at 220°C/425°F/ gas mark 7 oven for 30 minutes until golden. • Serve hot or cold.

Partridge en Croûte

An especially festive pastry dish which can also be served as a starter for a large gathering

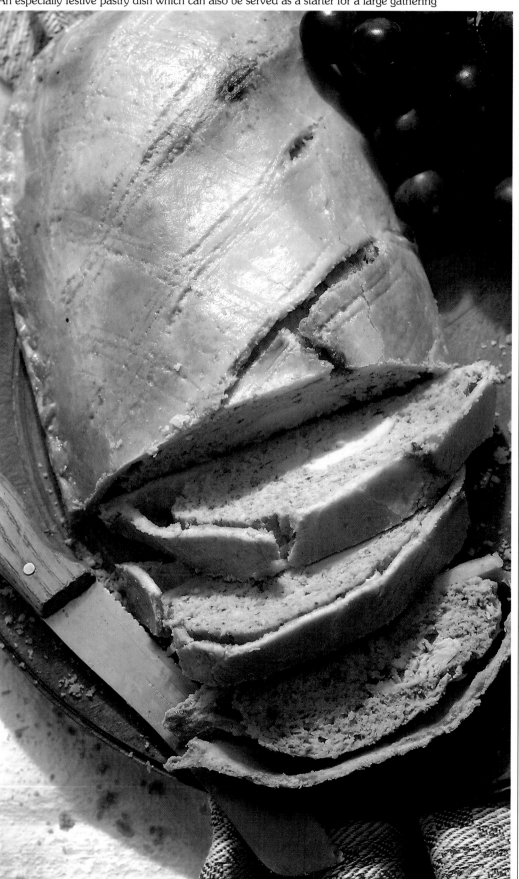

To serve 6:

2 x 600g/1¼ lb roast partridges

2 shallots • 100g/4oz mushrooms

1 tbsp finely chopped fresh basil

300g/10oz minced veal or sausagemeat

1 egg

125ml/4fl oz crème fraîche

Pinch hot paprika

Pinch ginger • Salt

FOR THE PASTRY:

250g/8oz flour • 100g/4oz butter

Salt • 2 eggs

Preparation time: 40 minutes
Baking time: 45 minutes
Nutritional value:
Analysis per serving, approx:
• 3360kJ/800kcal • 56g protein
• 53g fat • 35g carbohydrate

First make the pastry dough. Sift together the flour and a pinch of salt. Dice the butter and rub into the flour with the fingertips until the mixture resembles fine breadcrumbs. Lightly beat 1 egg, and mix lightly into the dough until it forms a ball. Place in a bowl, cover, and set aside to rest in the refrigerator. • Skin the partridges and slice the breast meat. Cut the remaining meat from the bones and finely dice. • Peel and finely chop the shallots. Finely chop the mushrooms. • Mix together the diced partridge meat, shallots, mushrooms and basil. Add the veal or sausagemeat, the egg, crème fraîche, paprika and ginger, and season to taste with salt. Mix well. • Halve the dough. Roll out each piece on a lightly floured work-surface into a rectangle measuring 15 x 30cm/6 x 12 inches. • Place half of the filling on 1 dough rectangle. Place the breast meat along the centre and cover with the remaining filling. Dampen the edges of the dough with water and lay the other dough rectangle over the top. Press the edges together firmly. Prick the top with a fork or lightly mark a criss-cross pattern across the top with a fork if liked. Beat the remaining egg, and brush over the top of the parcel. Transfer to a lightly-greased baking sheet. • Bake in a preheated oven at 200°C/400°F/gas mark 6 for 45 minutes.

Chicken Liver Terrine

An impressive but easy dish – even quicker with ready-made pork sausagemeat

To serve 6:

600g/1¼ lbs chicken livers
175g/6oz thinly sliced rindless bacon
2 thyme sprigs
2 rosemary sprigs
2 onions
25g/1oz dried ceps
½ tsp dried thyme
½ tsp dried rosemary
½ tsp ground cloves
½ tsp ground cinnamon
½ tsp ground mace
½ tsp ground ginger
5 tbsps medium sherry
Salt
500g/1lb 2oz minced veal or sausagemeat
200ml/7fl oz crème fraîche
2 tbsps finely chopped fresh parsley
3 bay leaves
2l/3½ pints boiling water

Preparation time: 1 hour
Cooking time: 45 minutes
Nutritional value:

Analysis per serving, approx:
• 3080kJ/735kcal
• 35g protein
• 60g fat
• 7g carbohydrate

Wash the chicken livers and pat dry. Cut off any yellowish or greenish portions or bits of fat from the livers. • Reserve 4 slices of the bacon and finely dice the remainder. Wash the thyme and rosemary sprigs carefully, shake dry and set aside. Peel and finely chop the onions. • Heat a small frying pan, and fry the diced bacon until the fat runs. Add the onions, and fry until transparent. Add the chicken livers, and stir-fry for 3 minutes until lightly browned. Add the ceps, dried thyme, dried rosemary, cloves, cinnamon, mace, ginger and sherry, and season to taste with salt. Fry for a

further 1 minute, stirring the mixture constantly. Remove from the heat and set aside to cool. • Roughly chop the livers. Mix the chopped livers, the veal or sausagemeat, crème fraîche and chopped parsley together throughly. Season to taste with salt. • Spoon the mixture into an ovenproof terrine or loaf tin and smooth the top. Place the thyme and rosemary sprigs and the bay leaves on top of the mixture and cover with the reserved bacon slices. • Cover the terrine with a double layer of aluminium foil and seal the edges. Place in a large ovenproof dish or roasting tin. Add enough boiling water to come halfway up the sides of the terrine or loaf tin. • Cook in a preheated oven at 175°C/350°F/ gas mark 4 for 45 minutes. • Remove from the oven and set aside to cool. Serve in slices or scoop out with a spoon. • Accompany with Cumberland sauce and freshly-baked baguette.

Our tip: For a finely textured terrine, combine the livers, veal or sausage meat, crème fraîche and chopped parsley in a liquidizer or food processor.

Duck and Mushroom Pie

Just the right thing as a special treat for good friends

Makes 1 x 26cm/8-inch pie
To serve 12:
2.5l/4½ pints water
Salt and freshly ground white pepper
1 x 2kg/4½ lb duck, with giblets
1 onion
2 cloves
1 bouquet garni
½ bay leaf
100g/4oz mushrooms
60g/2½oz butter
3 tbsps flour
2 egg yolks
½ tsp dried thyme
1 egg white
FOR THE PASTRY:
150g/5oz butter
350g/11oz flour
Salt
1 egg yolk, lightly beaten
8-10 tbsps iced water

Preparation time: 2½ hours
Baking time: 1 hour

Nutritional value:
Analysis per serving, approx:
- 2600kJ/620kcal
- 35g protein
- 44g fat
- 24g carbohydrate

First make the pastry dough. Dice the butter. Sift the flour and a pinch of salt onto a clean work surface, and make a hollow in the centre. Distribute the butter around the edge of the flour and pour the egg yolk and water into the hollow. Mix together with your fingers, pulling from the edges into the centre until the dough forms a ball. Place in a bowl, cover, and set aside to rest in the refrigerator. • Make the filling. Place the water in a large pan with a pinch of salt, and bring to the boil. Wash the duck and the giblets and reserve the liver. Add the duck and the remaining giblets to the boiling water. Lower the heat, and simmer for 30 minutes, skimming frequently. • Peel and halve the

onion. Stud 1 half of the onion with the cloves. Add both onion halves, the cloves, bouquet garni and bay leaf to the pan, and simmer for a further 1 hour. • Remove the duck from the pan and set aside to cool. Strain the stock, and set aside to cool. • Skim off the fat and reserve 250ml/8fl oz of stock. Skin the duck and cut the meat from the bones. Finely chop the duck meat. • Finely dice the duck liver. Finely chop the mushrooms. • Melt 50g/2oz of the butter, and fry the liver and the mushrooms until lightly browned. Stir in the flour, and cook, stirring constantly, for 3 minutes or until golden. Gradually stir in the reserved stock, and bring to the boil, stirring constantly. Lower the heat and cook, stirring constantly, for 5 minutes. Remove from the heat and allow to cool slightly. Stir in 1 egg yolk and the thyme, and season to taste with salt and pepper. Add the duck meat. •

Whisk the egg white until stiff, and fold into the filling. • Grease a 26cm/8-inch flan tin or dish with the remaining butter. • Halve the dough and roll out 1 piece on a lightly-floured work surface until it is a little larger than the flan tin. Line the tin with the dough, easing it carefully with your fingers. Prick the base with a fork. • Spoon in the filling and smooth the top. Dampen the edges of the dough with water. Roll out the other half of the dough until it is a little larger than the flan tin. Lift the dough over the filling. Press the edges together firmly to seal, and trim to fit. Make a decorative edging using a fork and prick the top. Make a decorative diamond pattern, if liked. • Beat the remaining egg yolk, and brush over the top of the pie. • Bake in a preheated oven at 220°C/425°F/gas mark 7 for 1 hour. Allow to cool in the tin.

Goose in Aspic

An unusual but delicious way of serving goose – a good dish to make when entertaining guests

To serve 6:

1 x 3kg/6³/₄ lb goose, with giblets
500g/1lb 2oz veal bones
2 onions
4 red peppers
2 carrots
2 celery stalks
Peel 1 lemon
1 bay leaf
2 cloves
4 peppercorns
¹/₂ tsp dried thyme
Pinch dried basil
Pinch dried tarragon
Salt
500ml/16fl oz vinegar
1.75l/3 pints boiling water
1 bouquet garni
45g/1¹/₂ oz powdered gelatine
Bunch of curly parsley

Preparation time: 1 hour
Cooking time: 2 hours
Setting time: 4 hours
Nutritional value:

Analysis per serving, approx:
- 5290kJ/1260kcal
- 60g protein
- 98g fat
- 3g carbohydrate

Separate the drumsticks from the goose. Cut the body into 4 pieces. Wash the goose pieces, giblets and veal bones. • Peel and chop the onions. Halve, seed, wash and dice the peppers. Peel the carrots. Trim and halve the celery stalks. • Place the goose pieces, giblets, veal bones, onions, peppers, carrots and celery in a large pan. Add the lemon peel, bay leaf, cloves, peppercorns, thyme, basil and tarragon, and season to taste with salt. Pour over the vinegar. • Cover with boiling water and bring to the boil. Skim several times. Lower the heat, cover and simmer for 1 hour. • Add the bouquet garni, and simmer for a further 1 hour. • Remove the goose pieces, carrots and celery and set aside. • Strain

the stock, and set aside to cool. Skim off the fat. • Skin the goose pieces and cut the meat from the bones. Dice the meat. • Slice the carrot, and cut the celery into matchstick strips. • Sprinkle the gelatine onto a small bowl of hot water. Set aside for 5 minutes to soften. Heat 5 tbsps of the reserved stock in a pan. Stir the gelatine, and add to the hot stock, in a continuous stream, stirring constantly. Add the remaining stock, stir and season to taste with salt and pepper. Set aside to cool. • Wash the parsley and shake dry. Pull off the leaves and discard the stalks. • Rinse out a large mould with cold water, and pour in a thin layer of aspic. Put the aspic in the refrigerator to set. • Arrange some parsley and a few vegetable slices over the aspic. Cover with a further layer of aspic, and return to the refrigerator to set. • Make a second layer of goose meat, vegetables and parsley, cover with aspic and return to the refrigerator

to set. Continue making layers in this way until all the ingredients are used up. • Finally, return to the refrigerator for a further 4 hours or until completely set. • Before serving, loosen the edge of the aspic from the bowl using a sharp, heated knife. Plunge the bowl briefly into hot water and turn out the aspic onto a plate. • Can be served with roast potatoes and sweet and sour salad made from beetroot or wax beans.

Chicken and Fennel Tartlets

Excellent with a fine rosé wine

To make 6

400g/14oz fennel	
125ml/4fl oz chicken stock	
400g/14oz cooked boneless chicken • 1 tbsp olive oil	
1 tbsp lemon juice	
1 tbsp mayonnaise	
1/2 tsp mild paprika	
Pinch of cayenne • 1 lemon	

FOR THE PASTRY:

100g/4oz butter, diced
200g/7oz wholemeal flour
Pinch of ground aniseed
Pinch of ground fennel seeds
1/2 tsp baking powder
Salt and freshly ground pepper
2 x size 3 eggs, lightly beaten

Preparation time: 1¹/₂ hours
Nutritional value:

Analysis per tartlet, approx:
• 1600kJ/380kcal • 18g protein
• 22g fat • 27g carbohydrate

Make a dough with the butter, flour, aniseed, fennel seeds, baking powder, a pinch of salt and pepper and the eggs. Knead lightly until smooth. Trim and wash the fennel, reserving the feathery leaves. Cut the fennel into matchstick strips. • Place the chicken stock in a pan, bring to the boil and add the fennel strips. Lower the heat, cover and simmer for 15 minutes. Drain and set aside. • Grease 6 x 8cm/3 inch tartlet tins. • Roll out the dough on a lightly floured work surface. Cut out 6 circles, slightly larger than the tins. Line the tins with the dough circles, prick the bases, and bake in a preheated oven at 180°C/350°F/gas mark 4 for 15 minutes. • Remove the pastry cases from the tins and transfer carefully to a wire rack to cool. • Dice the chicken and mix with the fennel, oil, lemon juice, mayonnaise, paprika and cayenne. • Slice the lemon. • Fill the tartlet cases with the chicken and fennel mixture, and garnish with the lemon slices and reserved fennel leaves.

Chicken and Grape Tartlets

A welcome late-evening snack

To make 6:

400g/14oz cooked skinless, boneless chicken
Salt and freshly ground white pepper
500g/1lb 2oz white grapes
8 gherkins
100g/4oz full fat soft cheese
6 tbsps crème fraîche
2 tbsps tomato purée
1/4 tsp dried basil
15g/1/2 oz butter
18 basil leaves, to garnish

FOR THE PASTRY:

100g/4oz butter, diced
200g/7oz wholemeal flour
1/2 tsp baking powder
Salt
2 x size 3 eggs, lightly beaten

Preparation time: 1 hour
Nutritional value:

Analysis per tartlet, approx:
• 2400kJ/570kcal• 30g protein
• 35g fat• 35g carbohydrate

Make a dough with the butter, flour, baking powder, a pinch of salt and eggs. Mix together with your fingers, pulling the ingredients from the outside to the centre. • Finely dice the chicken, and season to taste with salt and pepper. Halve and seed the grapes. Finely dice the gherkins. • Beat together the soft cheese, crème fraîche, tomato purée and basil. Stir in the gherkins, grapes and chicken. • Grease 6 x 8cm/3-inch tartlet tins with the butter. • Roll out the dough on a lightly-floured work surface. Cut out 6 circles, slightly larger than the tins. Line the tartlet tins with the dough circles. Prick the bases lightly with a fork. Bake in a preheated oven at 180°C/350°F/gas mark 4 for 15 minutes. • Remove the pastry cases from the tins, and transfer carefully to a wire rack to cool. • Fill with the chicken and grape mixture and garnish with the basil leaves.

Chicken Croissants

These rough puff pastry croissants are tasty either hot or cold, served with a salad and wine

To make 10:

400g/14oz skinless chicken fillets
200g/7oz mushrooms
2 onions
50g/1oz butter
1 tsp dried thyme
Salt and freshly ground white pepper
2 tbsps double cream
1 egg
1 tbsp condensed milk
5 sheets frozen rough puff pastry, thawed

Preparation time: 1 hour
Baking time: 20 minutes
Nutritional value:

Analysis per croissant, approx:
- 800kJ/190kcal
- 12g protein
- 11g fat
- 12g carbohydrate

Wash the chicken fillets and pat dry. Finely dice. Finely chop the mushrooms. Peel and finely chop the onions. • Melt the butter, and fry the onions until transparent. Add the mushrooms, and thyme, and season to taste with salt and pepper. Cook, stirring frequently, until the liquid has evaporated. Remove the mixture from the heat, stir in the cream and set aside to cool. • Separate the egg. Stir the egg white and the chopped chicken into the mushroom mixture. • Beat together the egg yolk and the condensed milk. • Rinse a baking sheet with cold water. • Cut the pastry sheets in half diagonally, and roll out each triangle widthways on a lightly floured work-surface. Divide the filling among the triangles, and roll up from the long side. Bend into croissant shapes. Brush the croissants with the egg yolk and condensed milk mixture and place on the baking sheet. • Bake in a preheated oven at 200°C/400°F/gas mark 6 for 20 minutes until golden.

Quail with Truffle Stuffing

A delicacy for a champagne breakfast

4 quails
Salt and freshly ground white pepper
200g/7oz goose livers
40g/1½ oz butter
2 tbsps Madeira
2 tsps bottled truffle pieces
1 tbsp finely chopped fresh basil
2 tbsps dry breadcrumbs
½ head endive
2 small seedless mandarins
2 tbsps orange juice
1 tbsp olive oil
2 basil sprigs

Preparation time: 1¼ hours
Nutritional value:
Analysis per serving, approx:
- 2940kJ/700kcal
- 34g protein
- 59g fat
- 12g carbohydrate

Wash the quails and pat dry. Rub the inside with salt and pepper. • Wash the goose livers and pat dry. Trim and dice. • Melt 15g/½oz of the butter, and stir-fry the livers until lightly browned. Add 1 tbsp of the Madeira, and season to taste with salt and pepper. Cook, stirring constantly, for 5 minutes. Remove the pan from the heat. • Finely chop the truffles. Mix together the liver, truffles, chopped basil and breadcrumbs. • Spoon the stuffing into the quails and close with trussing thread. • Melt the remaining butter in a roasting tin over a medium heat, and fry the quails until browned all over. Roast in a preheated oven at 200°C/400°F/gas mark 6 for 20 minutes. Transfer to a serving dish, remove the trussing thread and set aside to cool. • Wash, shake dry and shred the endive. Peel the mandarins, divide into segments and remove the membrane. • Mix together the orange juice, remaining Madeira and olive oil, and season to taste with salt. Mix together the endive and mandarins, pour over the dressing and toss lightly. • Arrange on the serving dish with the quails and garnish with the basil sprigs.

Poultry – with a Difference

Delicious winter combinations with Brussels sprouts and broccoli

Chicken with Broccoli
Illustrated left

1 x 1.2 kg/2½ lb chicken
1 carrot • 1 onion • 1 celery stalk
2 tbsps sunflower oil
3 tbsps sherry vinegar
250ml/8fl oz water
1 sprig thyme
Salt and freshly ground white pepper • 8 shallots
800g/1½ lbs broccoli
15g/½ oz butter • 1 tsp sugar
5 tbsps orange juice
4 tbsps corn oil

Preparation time: 1 hour
Cooking time: 30 minutes
Nutritional value:
Analysis per serving, approx:
• 2800kJ/670kcal • 72g protein
• 36g fat • 23g carbohydrate

Wash the chicken and pat dry. Cut into 8 pieces. • Peel and chop the carrot. Peel and chop the onion. Trim, wash and chop the celery. • Heat the sunflower oil, and fry the chicken pieces until browned all over. Add the carrot, onion and celery, and fry, stirring constantly, until lightly browned. Add the vinegar, water and thyme, and season to taste with salt. Bring to the boil. Lower the heat, cover and simmer for 30 minutes. • Remove the chicken pieces and set aside. Strain the stock and discard the vegetables. Return the stock to the pan, and bring to the boil. Peel the shallots, add to the stock and boil for 10 minutes. Remove the shallots and set aside. • Trim and wash the broccoli and divide into florets. In a separate pan, bring 500ml/16fl oz water to the boil, add the broccoli and cook for 10 minutes. Remove the broccoli and set aside to cool. • Melt the butter, stir in the sugar and cook gently, stirring constantly, until the sugar has dissolved. Add the shallots, and coat thoroughly to glaze. • Mix together the orange juice and corn oil, and season. Toss the broccoli in the orange juice mixture and arrange on a serving dish with the chicken and glazed shallots.

Goose with Brussels Sprout Salad
Illustrated right

4 x 350g/11oz goose drumsticks
1 carrot • 1 onion
3 tbsps sunflower oil • Salt
750ml/1¼ pints hot chicken stock
6 tbsps white wine vinegar
6 tbsps medium sherry
800g/1½ lbs Brussels sprouts
1 large tart dessert apple
2 tsps lemon juice
2 tbsps olive oil • Pinch of sugar
1 tbsp finely chopped fresh parsley

Preparation time: 45 minutes
Cooking time: 40 minutes

Nutritional value:
Analysis per serving, approx:
• 2700kJ/640kcal • 86g protein
• 24g fat • 19g carbohydrate

Wash the goose drumsticks and pat dry. Peel and chop the carrot. Peel and quarter the onion. • Heat the sunflower oil, and fry the drumsticks until brown. Add the carrot and onion, season to taste with salt and stir-fry until lightly browned. Add the stock, vinegar and sherry, and bring to the boil. Lower the heat, cover and simmer for 40 minutes. Remove the drumsticks and set aside to cool. Strain the stock and discard the vegetables. Return the stock to the pan, bring to the boil and allow to reduce to 250ml/8fl oz. Set aside to cool. • Trim, wash and boil the Brussels sprouts. Drain and cool. • Peel, core and dice the apple. Mix together the lemon juice, olive oil, sugar, parsley, reduced stock, Brussels sprouts and diced apple.

Tender Poultry Breast with Delicious Salads

These recipes use the best on offer in the winter

Larded Turkey Breast
Illustrated right

50g/2oz rindless streaky bacon

1kg/2¼ lbs turkey breast in one piece

2 tsps mild paprika

Salt and freshly ground white pepper

6 tbsps light white wine

2 small radicchio heads

200g/7oz fresh pineapple

2 tsps lemon juice

2 tsps clear honey

Preparation time: 40 minutes
Cooking time: 40 minutes
Nutritional value:
Analysis per serving, approx:
• 1700kJ/400kcal • 60g protein
• 11g fat • 12g carbohydrate

Cut the bacon into 5mm/¼-inch strips. Place in the freezer to harden. • Wash the turkey breast and pat dry. • Using a larding needle, thread the bacon strips evenly through the turkey breast. Rub the meat with the paprika, and season to taste with salt and pepper. Place on a large sheet of foil and pour over 4 tbsps of the wine. Seal the parcel, prick the top several times with a needle and roast in a preheated oven at 200°C/400°F/gas mark 6 for 40 minutes. Remove from the foil, transfer to a dish and allow to cool. Reserve the roasting juices and set aside to cool. • Wash the radicchio, shake dry, and separate the leaves. Arrange on a serving dish, and season to taste with salt and pepper. • Peel, core and dice the pineapple. Arrange on the dish with the radicchio, and sprinkle over the lemon juice. Heat the remaining wine, and stir in the honey until dissolved. Remove from the heat and allow to cool slightly. Drizzle over the radicchio. • Carve the turkey breast in thin slices and arrange with the radicchio and pineapple. Sprinkle the cold roasting juices over the meat.

Duck Breast with Chicory Salad
Illustrated left

2 x 300g/10oz duck breasts with skin

25g/1oz butter

Salt and freshly ground white pepper

3 chicory heads

2 tomatoes

200g/7oz courgettes

1 onion

1 tbsp lemon juice

1 tbsp maple syrup

2 tbsps walnut oil

1 tbsp snipped chives

Preparation time: 20 minutes
Nutritional value:
Analysis per serving, approx:

• 1400kJ/330kcal
• 40g protein
• 11g fat
• 21g carbohydrate

Wash the duck breast and pat dry. Melt the butter, and fry the duck breast for 15 minutes on each side until cooked through. Season to taste with salt and pepper, and set aside to cool. • Trim and wash the chicory and pat dry. Reserve a few whole leaves for the garnish, and slice the remainder into rings. • Skin and finely chop the tomatoes. Peel and dice the courgettes. Peel and finely chop the onion. • Mix together the chicory slices, tomatoes, courgettes, onion, lemon juice, maple syrup and oil, and season to taste with salt. Arrange on a serving dish and sprinkle over the chives. • Carve the duck breast in thin slices and arrange on the dish with the salad. Garnish with the reserved chicory leaves.

Unusual Salads

One with glazed chestnuts, the other with kiwi fruit

Breast of Pheasant in Bacon
Illustrated left

2 x 1kg/2¹/₄ lbs pheasants	
Salt and freshly ground white pepper	
1 tsp dried sage	
40g/1¹/₂ oz butter	
50g/2oz very thinly sliced rindless streaky bacon	
250g/8oz sweet chestnuts	
2 tsps sugar	

Preparation time: 1 hour
Nutritional value:
Analysis per serving, approx:
• 3300kJ/790kcal • 81g protein
• 42g fat • 31g carbohydrate

Wash the pheasants and pat dry. Rub the insides with salt and pepper. Crush half the sage, and divide between the insides of the pheasants. • Melt 25g/1oz of the butter, and fry the pheasants for 5 minutes until browned all over. • Place, breast side up, in a roasting tin. Pour over the melted butter and wrap in the bacon slices. Roast in a preheated oven at 220°C/425°F/gas mark 7 for 30 minutes. Remove from the oven, transfer to a dish and set aside to cool. • Using a small, sharp knife, cut a cross in the pointed ends of the chestnuts, place in a pan and cover with water. Bring to the boil and cook for 20 minutes. • Rinse the chestnuts in cold water and peel. • Melt the remaining butter in a pan, add the sugar, and cook gently, stirring constantly, until the sugar has dissolved. Coat the chestnuts in the mixture to glaze and set aside to cool. • Cut the breast from the pheasants and carve into 1cm/¹/₂-inch thick slices, together with the bacon. Arrange on a serving dish with the chestnuts and sprinkle over the remaining sage. (Use the remaining pheasant meat in other recipes.)

Chicken Breast with Kiwi Fruit
Illustrated right

800g/1¹/₂ lbs chicken breast	
1 l/1³/₄ pints chicken stock	
1 leek	
1 celery stalk	
4 kiwi fruit	
1 orange	
1 lemon	
15g/¹/₂ oz butter	
1 tbsp sugar	
Pinch cayenne	
Salt	

Preparation time: 45 minutes
Nutritional value:
Analysis per serving, approx:
• 1300kJ/310kcal • 49g protein
• 5g fat • 21g carbohydrate

Wash the chicken breast. Place the chicken stock in a pan and bring to the boil. Add the chicken, and cook for 10 minutes, skimming frequently. • Trim, wash and slice the leek. Trim, wash and slice the celery. Add to the stock, lower the heat and poach for a further 10 minutes. The surface of the water should be barely rippling. • Peel the kiwi fruit and cut into 5mm/¹/₄-inch slices. Arrange the kiwi fruit on a serving dish. • Wash the orange in hot water and dry. Thinly pare half the peel from the orange. Cut the peel into thin strips and set aside. • Squeeze the lemon and the orange. • Melt the butter in a small pan, add the sugar, and cook gently, stirring constantly, until the sugar has dissolved. Stir in the fruit juice, bring to the boil and allow to reduce to about 2 tbsps of liquid. Add the cayenne pepper, and season to taste with salt. Allow to cool and pour over the kiwi fruit. • Skin and bone the chicken breast. Carve into slices and arrange on the kiwi. Sprinkle with the reserved orange peel.

Chicken with Spicy Dressings

Picnic ideas – delicious with chilled white wine

Chicken with Anchovy Mayonnaise
Illustrated right

1 x 1.2kg/2½ lb chicken
1 bunch parsley
3 basil sprigs
1 bouquet garni
1 onion
1 clove • 1 bay leaf
100g/4oz canned tuna, drained
4 anchovy fillets • 1 tbsp capers
1 gherkin • 4 tbsps mayonnaise
1 tsp lemon juice
Salt and freshly ground white pepper • 1 lemon
Lettuce leaves, to garnish

Preparation time: 30 minutes
Cooking time: 1½ hours
Cooling time: 2 hours
Nutritional value:
Analysis per serving, approx:
• 2300kJ/550kcal • 71g protein
• 30g fat • 3g carbohydrate

Wash the chicken and place in large pan. • Wash the parsley, remove the leaves and set aside, reserving the stalks. Wash the basil sprigs and add to the pan, together with the bouquet garni and reserved parsley stalks. Peel and halve the onion. Stud one half of the onion with the clove and place both onion halves and the bay leaf in the pan. Cover with boiling water. • Cook the chicken for 30 minutes, skimming frequently. Lower the heat, and poach the chicken for a further 1 hour. The surface of the water should be barely rippling. • Remove from the heat and set aside to cool in the stock. • Finely chop the tuna, anchovy fillets, capers and gherkin, and mix together. Stir the anchovy mixture into the mayonnaise. Add the lemon juice, and season to taste with salt and pepper. Finely chop the parsley leaves, and stir into the anchovy mayonnaise. • Remove the chicken from the pan, skin and cut the meat from the bones. Slice the meat and arrange on a serving dish. Cut the lemon into wedges. • Serve with the anchovy mayonnaise and garnish with the lemon wedges and lettuce leaves.

Chicken in Tarragon Sauce
Illustrated left

2 garlic cloves
1 x 1.2kg/2½ lb chicken
4 tbsps olive oil • 2 bay leaves
Juice 1 lemon
250ml/8fl oz dry white wine
4 tbsps tarragon vinegar
Salt and freshly ground white pepper
1 tbsp chopped fresh tarragon
12 black olives, to garnish
1 tbsp coarsely chopped peanuts

Preparation time: 20 minutes
Cooking time: 40 minutes
Cooling time: 1 hour
Nutritional value:
Analysis per serving, approx:
• 2400kJ/570kcal • 62g protein
• 33g fat • 5g carbohydrate

Peel and finely chop the garlic. Wash the chicken and pat dry. Cut into 8 pieces. • Heat the oil, and fry the chicken pieces until browned all over. Add the garlic and the bay leaves, and stir-fry until the onion is lightly browned. Sprinkle over the lemon juice. Add the wine and vinegar, and season to taste with salt and pepper. Bring to the boil. Lower the heat, cover, and simmer for 40 minutes, turning the chicken pieces frequently. • Remove the chicken and set aside. • Bring the cooking juices to the boil and allow to reduce. Set aside to cool. • Arrange the chicken pieces on a plate, drizzle over the cold cooking juices and sprinkle over the tarragon. Serve garnished with the olives and chopped peanuts.

Marinated Chicken Drumsticks

A meal for hot days – serve with a baguette and the same white wine as used in the marinade

2 garlic cloves
1 small chilli
250ml/8fl oz dry white wine
1 tbsp wholegrain mustard
1 tsp herbes de Provence (thyme, rosemary, bay leaf, basil and savory)
Salt and freshly ground black pepper
8 x 150g/5oz chicken drumsticks
6 tbsps olive oil

Preparation time: 15 minutes
Marinating time: 3 hours
Cooking time: 45 minutes
Nutritional value:
Analysis per serving, approx:
• 1900kJ/450kcal
• 62g protein
• 17g fat
• 3g carbohydrate

Peel and finely chop the garlic. Trim and seed the chilli. Wash, pat dry and slice into thin rings. Mix together the garlic, chilli, wine, mustard and herbs, and season to taste with pepper. • Wash the chicken drumsticks and pat dry. Rub with salt and place in a shallow dish. Pour over the marinade, and set aside in the refrigerator to marinate for 3 hours, turning the drumsticks frequently. • Drain the drumsticks and reserve the marinade. • Arrange the drumsticks in an ovenproof dish, and brush with the oil. Roast in a preheated oven at 200°C/400°F/gas mark 6 for 35 minutes, basting frequently with the reserved marinade. • Increase the oven temperature to 240°C/475°F/gas mark 9, and roast the drumsticks for a further 10 minutes until crisp and golden. Remove from the oven and set aside to cool. • Serve the drumsticks in the sauce.

Stuffed Turkey Fillet

Suitable as the main dish of a cold buffet

To serve 8:
400g/14oz spinach
2 onions
2 garlic cloves
1 thick slice stale bread, crusts removed
2 tbsps olive oil
50g/2oz freshly grated Parmesan cheese
50g/2oz cream cheese
1 egg
2 tbsps breadcrumbs
2 tbsps flaked almonds
$\frac{1}{2}$ tsp dried oregano
Pinch of ground nutmeg
Salt and freshly ground black pepper
1.5kg/3lbs 6oz turkey breast in one piece
$\frac{1}{2}$ tsp dried thyme
4 tbsps sunflower oil
125ml/4fl oz boiling water
200g/7oz mushrooms
2 shallots
15g/$\frac{1}{2}$oz butter
2 tbsps finely chopped fresh parsley
250ml/8fl oz double cream
250ml/8fl oz crème fraîche

Preparation time: 1 hour
Cooking time: 1$\frac{1}{2}$ hours
Relaxing time: 6 hours
Nutritional value:

Analysis per serving, approx:
- 2500kJ/600kcal
- 54g protein
- 35g fat
- 16g carbohydrate

Trim and wash the spinach. Place in a pan and cook for 5 minutes in the water still clinging to the leaves. Drain, squeeze out excess water and finely chop. • Peel and chop the onions. Peel and finely chop the garlic. • Tear the bread into pieces and place in a bowl. Cover with cold water and set aside to soak. • Heat the olive oil, and fry the onion and garlic for 5 minutes or until transparent but not browned. Add the spinach, and stir-fry until all the liquid has evaporated. Transfer to a bowl. • Squeeze out the bread. Mix together the spinach, Parmesan cheese, cream cheese, egg, breadcrumbs, flaked almonds, oregano and nutmeg, and season to taste with salt and pepper. • Wash the turkey breast and pat dry. Using trussing thread, sew up the places in the meat where the bones were removed. Cut a deep pocket in the meat and spoon in the spinach stuffing. Sew the meat together with trussing thread. • Rub with salt and pepper, sprinkle over the thyme and place in a roasting tin. • Heat the sunflower oil, and pour over the turkey. Roast in a preheated oven at 200°C/400°F/gas mark 6 for 1$\frac{1}{2}$ hours, frequently pouring a little hot water around the turkey and basting the meat with the roasting juices. • Remove the turkey from the roasting tin and wrap in foil.

When cold, set aside in the refrigerator to rest for 6 hours. • Make the sauce. Thinly slice the mushrooms. Peel and finely chop the shallots. • Melt the butter, and stir-fry the mushrooms for 3 minutes over a high heat. Add the shallots and parsley, and stir-fry until browned. Season with salt and pepper to taste and remove from the heat. Stir in the cream and crème fraîche. Transfer to a sauce boat, cover and set aside in the refrigerator. • Remove the turkey from the foil and take out the trussing thread. Carve the turkey in thick slices and hand the sauce separately.

Savoury Toppers

Freshly baked crackers with a delicious topping make delightful canapés

To make 25:

200g/7oz turkey or chicken livers
1 onion • 25g/1oz butter
Sea salt and freshly ground black pepper • 3 tbsps double cream
¹/₂ tsp finely chopped fresh thyme
¹/₂ tsp finely chopped fresh marjoram
2 tsps finely chopped fresh parsley • 7 cherry tomatoes
25 fresh basil or marjoram leaves

FOR THE CRACKERS:

200g/7oz wholemeal flour
Pinch curry powder
Pinch mild paprika
¹/₂ tsp baking powder
Salt and freshly ground white pepper • 100g/4oz butter
1 egg • 2 tbsps sesame seeds

Preparation time: 45 minutes
Baking time: 10 minutes
Nutritional value:
Analysis per cracker, approx:
• 340kJ/81kcal • 3g protein
• 5g fat • 5g carbohydrate

Sift the flour with the curry powder, paprika, baking powder and a pinch of salt and pepper. Dice 100g/4oz of the butter, and distribute around the edge of the flour. Break the egg into the flour. Mix to a dough with your hands, pulling the ingredients from the outside. Shape the dough into a roll 5cm/2 inches across and 15cm/6 inches long. Trim and chop the livers. Peel and finely chop the onion. • Melt half the butter, and fry the onion until lightly browned. Add the livers, cover, and fry for 5 minutes. Season, and set aside to cool. • Purée the cooled livers with the frying juices, cream, thyme and marjoram. Stir in the parsley, and season. • Grease a baking sheet with the remaining butter. • Cut the roll of dough into 5mm/¹/₄ inch slices, and place on the baking sheet. Sprinkle over the sesame seeds and press down gently. Bake in a preheated oven at 200°C/400°F/gas mark 6 for 10 minutes until golden. • Transfer to a wire rack, and set aside to cool. • Spread the crackers with the paste, and garnish with the tomatoes and basil or marjoram.

Mango and Turkey Salad

Unusual but very tasty

125g/5oz long-grain brown rice
475ml/15fl oz water
1 tsp whole cardamom seeds
1/2 tsp curry powder
Salt and freshly ground white pepper
3 x 150g/5oz turkey escalopes
Juice 1/2 lemon
1 x 300g/10oz ripe mango
2 tbsps crème fraîche
2 tbsps sesame oil
4 tbsps chicken stock
2 tbsps finely chopped fresh dill
4 tbsps sesame seeds
Lettuce leaves and dill, to garnish

Preparation time: 50 minutes
Nutritional value:
Analysis per serving, approx:
• 1800kJ/430kcal • 25g protein
• 21g fat • 37g carbohydrate

Wash the rice under cold running water. Place in a pan with the water, cardamom seeds and half the curry powder, and season to taste with salt. Bring to the boil. Stir once, reduce the heat, cover and simmer for 25 minutes. • Wash the turkey escalopes and pat dry. Sprinkle over half the lemon juice, and season to taste with pepper. • Place the escalopes on the rice, cover and cook for a further 5 minutes. Turn the escalopes, cover and cook for a further 5 minutes. • Remove the escalopes and set aside to cool. Drain the rice and set aside to cool. Cut the escalopes into strips. • Peel the mango. Chop half and slice the other half. • Mix the rice with the remaining lemon juice, remaining curry powder, turkey strips, chopped mango, crème fraîche, sesame oil, stock and dill, and season to taste with salt. • Dry-fry the sesame seeds until they change colour and give off a pleasant smell. • Arrange the rice salad on a dish and sprinkle over the sesame seeds. Garnish with lettuce, mango and dill.

Indian Rice Salad

For lovers of foreign food

125g/5oz long-grain brown rice
600ml/1 pint water
1 tsp vegetable stock granules
200g/7oz cooked chicken
2 bananas • 1 tsp lemon juice
150ml/5fl oz natural set yogurt
1 tbsp crème fraîche
1 tbsp sesame oil
2 tbsps white wine vinegar
125ml/4fl oz chicken stock
1 small red pepper • 1 onion
150g/5oz fresh, peeled pineapple
1-2 tsps freshly grated root ginger
1 tsp curry powder
Lemon balm sprig
Lettuce leaves
1 very small yellow pepper

Preparation time: 45 minutes
Nutritional value:
Analysis per serving, approx:
• 1300kJ/310kcal • 15g protein
• 8g fat • 45g carbohydrate

Wash the rice. Place in a saucepan with the water and stock granules, and bring to the boil. Stir, reduce the heat, cover and simmer for 35 minutes. • Cut the chicken into strips. Peel the bananas. Slice 1 banana and sprinkle with the lemon juice. Mash the other banana, and mix with the yogurt, crème fraîche, oil, vinegar and chicken stock. • Halve, seed and wash the red pepper. Chop most of the pepper and cut the rest into matchstick strips for the garnish. Peel and finely chop the onion. Finely dice the pineapple. Wash the lemon balm and pat dry. Coarsely chop half, and reserve the other half for the garnish. • Mix together the rice, chicken, diced pineapple, sliced banana, onion and chopped red pepper. Stir in the banana dressing, ginger, curry powder and chopped lemon balm, and season. Halve, seed and wash the yellow pepper. Cut into matchstick strips. • Garnish the rice salad with lettuce, pepper strips, lemon balm leaves, pineapple and banana.

Salads with a Special Touch

Poultry is ideal for tasty mixed salads

Quail Breasts with Mixed Leaves
Illustrated left

4 x 150g/5oz quails
4 black peppercorns
Salt and freshly ground black pepper
1 celery stalk
2 shallots
1 small head radicchio
1/4 head endive
100g/4oz lamb's lettuce
1 small orange
1 tbsp orange juice
1 tbsp sherry vinegar
2 tbsps olive oil
25g/1oz butter

Preparation time: 1 hour
Nutritional value:
Analysis per serving, approx:
- 1300kJ/310kcal
- 34g protein
- 17g fat
- 11g carbohydrate

Wash the quails. Place in a pan and cover with water. Add the peppercorns and a pinch of salt. Bring to the boil and skim. • Trim, wash and slice the celery. Peel and quarter the shallots. Add the celery and shallots to the pan, lower the heat and simmer gently for 30 minutes. The surface of the water should be barely rippling. • Remove the quails and set aside to cool. • Wash the radicchio and shake dry. Separate the leaves. Wash, shake dry and shred the endive. Wash the lamb's lettuce and shake dry. • Peel and slice the orange. Mix together the orange juice, vinegar and oil, and season to taste with salt and pepper. • Skin the quails and cut the meat from the bones, leaving the breasts whole. Finely chop the remaining meat. • Melt the butter, and fry the quail breasts for 1 minute on each side. Toss the remaining quail meat briefly in the hot butter. • Arrange the salad leaves and orange slices on a serving dish, sprinkle with the dressing and arrange the warm quail meat on top.

Chicken and Cornmeal Salad
Illustrated right

475ml/15fl oz water
1 tsp vegetable stock granules
100g/4oz coarse cornmeal
1 green pepper
1 red pepper
Salt and freshly ground black pepper
2 tomatoes
400g/14oz cooked chicken
2 tbsps olive oil
1-2 tbsps cider vinegar
1 tsp finely chopped fresh rosemary
1 tsp finely chopped fresh thyme
1/2 tsp mild paprika
2 tbsps snipped chives

Preparation time: 40 minutes
Cooking time: 1 hour
Nutritional value:
Analysis per serving, approx:
- 1100kJ/260kcal • 27g protein
- 5.5g fat • 25g carbohydrate

Place the water and stock granules in a pan, and bring to the boil. Gradually sprinkle over the cornmeal. Lower the heat and simmer very gently, stirring frequently, for 1 hour. • Halve, seed, wash and quarter the peppers. Blanch in boiling, lightly salted water for 5 minutes. Drain, refresh under cold water and cut into matchstick strips. • Skin and quarter the tomatoes. • Cut the chicken into matchstick strips. • Mix together the cooked cornmeal, oil, vinegar, rosemary, thyme, paprika, pepper strips and chicken, and season with pepper to taste. Arrange on a serving dish, garnish with the tomato quarters and sprinkle over the chives.

Poultry Salads with Fine Vegetables

Exquisite salads to spoil gourmets

Chicken and Asparagus Salad
Illustrated left

1 x 1kg/2¼ lb chicken, with giblets
Salt and freshly ground white pepper
½ onion • 1 clove
¼ bay leaf • 100g/4oz leeks
1 carrot • 1 celery stalk
1 kg/2¼ lbs green asparagus
2 tbsps apple vinegar
Pinch sugar • 4 tbsps corn oil
2 tbsps fresh chives

Preparation time: 40 minutes
Cooking time: 1¾ hours
Nutritional value:
Analysis per serving, approx:
• 2100kJ/500kcal • 58g protein
• 26g fat • 17g carbohydrate

Wash the chicken and the giblets. Place in a pan, cover with water and season to taste with salt. Bring to the boil and cook for 15 minutes, skimming frequently. Reduce the heat and simmer gently for 30 minutes. The surface of the water should be barely rippling. • Stud the onion half with the clove. • Trim, wash and chop the leeks. Peel and slice the carrot. Trim, wash and halve the celery. • Add the onion, clove, bay leaf, leeks, carrot and celery to the pan, and simmer gently for a further 1 hour. • Wash the asparagus, peel the stalks, cut off the tips and reserve. • Remove the chicken from the pan and set aside to cool. Strain the stock, discarding the giblets and the stock vegetables. Return the stock to the pan and bring to the boil. • Cut the asparagus stalks into 5cm/2-inch chunks. Add to the stock and cook for 8 minutes. Add the tips, and cook for a further 7 minutes. Remove the asparagus with a slotted spoon and set aside to cool. • Skin the chicken and cut the meat from the bones. Dice the meat. • Mix together the vinegar, sugar and oil, and season to taste with salt and pepper. Arrange the chicken and asparagus on a serving dish and pour over the dressing. Sprinkle over the chives.

Duck Breast with Chanterelle Salad
Illustrated right

300g/10oz duck fillet in one piece
½ tsp dried marjoram
Salt and freshly ground black pepper
4 tbsps walnut oil
200g/7oz chanterelles
25g/1oz rindless streaky bacon
1 small head oakleaf lettuce
2 shallots
4 tbsps balsamic or white wine vinegar

Preparation time: 45 minutes
Nutritional value:
Analysis per serving, approx:
• 960kJ/230kcal • 20g protein
• 14g fat • 5g carbohydrate

Wash the duck fillet and pat dry. Rub with the marjoram, and season with pepper to taste. Heat 1 tbsp of the oil, and fry the duck fillet for 5 minutes on each side. Remove from the pan and set aside to cool. • Wash the chanterelles and pat dry. Finely dice the bacon. • Fry the bacon in the same pan until golden. Add the chanterelles, and fry for 2 minutes. Remove the bacon and chanterelles from the pan and set aside to cool. • Thinly slice the duck fillet. • Wash the lettuce and shake dry. Separate the leaves. Peel and finely chop the shallots. Mix together the lettuce and shallots, pour over the vinegar and remaining oil, and season to taste with salt. Lightly toss. • Arrange the lettuce and shallots on a serving dish with the duck fillet, bacon and chanterelles on top.

Duck Liver and Red Cabbage Salad

An unusual mixture, with pears and sherry

400g/14oz duck livers
Pinch ground cinnamon
Pinch ground cloves
Pinch crushed coriander
Pinch dried thyme
500g/1lb 2oz red cabbage
5 tbsps red wine vinegar
4 tbsps sunflower oil
Salt and freshly ground white pepper
8 very thin slices rindless bacon
6 tbsps medium sherry
1 lettuce heart
2 tbsps double cream
1 tsp lemon juice
4 canned pear halves, drained
4 tsps redcurrant jelly

Preparation time: 50 minutes
Nutritional value:
Analysis per serving, approx:
• 1700kJ/400kcal
• 26g protein
• 23g fat
• 18g carbohydrate

Trim and wash the duck livers and pat dry. Cut into 2cm/³/₄-inch cubes. Add the cinnamon, ground cloves, coriander and thyme, stir and set aside. • Wash the red cabbage and shake dry. Shred finely and mash with a potato masher for 5 minutes. • Pour over the vinegar and oil, season to taste with salt, and toss lightly. Set aside. • Heat a pan, and dry-fry the bacon until crisp and brown. Remove from the pan and drain on kitchen paper. Fry the liver in the same pan for 5 minutes. Add 5 tbsps of the sherry, and season to taste with salt and pepper. Keep warm. • Wash the lettuce heart, shake dry and separate the leaves. • Mix together the cream, lemon juice and remaining sherry, and season to taste with salt and pepper. Arrange the lettuce leaves on a serving dish and sprinkle over the cream mixture. Arrange the red cabbage on top. Place the liver, with its juice, on the red cabbage. Crumble the bacon slices and sprinkle over the salad. Fill the pear halves with the redcurrant jelly and arrange on top of the salad.

Salad with Barley and Turkey

This salad of turkey, cereal and dried fruit is rich in nutritious ingredients

150g/5oz pearl barley

1l/1¾ pints water

1 x 800g/1½ lb turkey drumstick

Salt and freshly ground black pepper

2 tbsps finely chopped fresh mixed herbs

100g/4oz stoned prunes

50g/2oz leek

2 tsps vegetable stock granules

2 tbsps sunflower oil

2 tbsps crème fraîche

3 tbsps red wine vinegar

Lettuce leaves, to garnish

Soaking time: 12 hours
Preparation time: 30 minutes
Cooking time: 50 minutes
Nutritional value:
Analysis per serving, approx:
- 2100kJ/500 kcal
- 47g protein
- 15g fat
- 46g carbohydrate

Place the barley in a bowl, pour over the water, cover and leave to soak for 12 hours. • Transfer the barley and the soaking water to a large flameproof casserole. • Wash the turkey drumstick and pat dry. Rub with pepper. Place on top of the barley and bring to the boil over a medium heat. Lower the heat, cover and simmer for 30 minutes. Turn the drumstick over, add the mixed herbs and cook for a further 20 minutes, adding more water as necessary. • Remove the turkey drumstick and set aside to cool. Drain the barley and set aside to cool. • Skin the drumstick and cut the meat from the bone. Cut the meat into 3cm/1½-inch chunks. Season with pepper to taste. • Wash the prunes in warm water, pat dry and quarter. Trim and wash the leek and pat dry. Slice into very thin rings. • Bring 300ml/10fl oz water to the boil and dissolve the stock granules in it. • Mix together the barley, prunes, leek, turkey, stock, oil, crème fraîche and 2 tbsps of the vinegar, and season to taste with salt. • Pour over the remaining vinegar, and season again to taste with salt, if desired. Serve garnished with the lettuce leaves.

Main Course Salads

Scrumptious and filling ways with poultry

Potato Salad with Turkey Breast
Illustrated left

750g/1½ lbs waxy potatoes	
250ml/8fl oz chicken stock	
2 red onions	
2 ripe avocado pears	
Salt and freshly ground black pepper	
3-4 tbsps white wine vinegar	
2 tbsps sunflower oil	
300g/10oz smoked turkey breast	
2 tbsps chopped fresh dill	

Preparation time: 40 minutes
Cooking time: 30 minutes
Nutritional value:
Analysis per serving, approx:
• 2100kJ/500kcal
• 24g protein
• 28g fat
• 37g carbohydrate

Scrub the potatoes, place in a saucepan, cover with water and bring to the boil. Cover and cook for 30 minutes. • Bring the stock to the boil. • Peel, quarter and thinly slice the onions. • Peel, halve and stone the avocado pears. Cut in half lengthways once more and slice. • Drain the potatoes, rinse in cold water, peel and dice. Mix together the potatoes and hot chicken stock, and season to taste with pepper. Gently stir in the onion and avocado pears. Pour over the vinegar and oil, and season to taste with salt. Toss lightly. • Dice the turkey breast. Season the salad with salt to taste and add the turkey breast. Toss lightly. • Serve sprinkled with the dill.

Duck Salad
Illustrated right

75g/3oz whole oats	
475ml/15fl oz chicken stock	
400g/14oz savoy cabbage	
1l/1¾ pints water	
Salt and freshly ground black pepper	
1 red onion	
400g/14oz cooked duck fillet	
1 tbsp sunflower oil	
2 tbsps red wine vinegar	
1 tsp Worcestershire sauce	

Preparation time: 50 minutes
Nutritional value:
Analysis per serving, approx:
• 1800kJ/430kcal
• 26g protein
• 22g fat
• 30g carbohydrate

Place the oats and chicken stock in a pan, and bring to the boil. Boil for 5 minutes, lower the heat, cover and simmer gently for 40 minutes. • Meanwhile, wash the cabbage, discarding the stalk and tough outer leaves. Shake dry and finely shred. Place the water in a pan and bring to the boil. Add a pinch of salt and blanch the cabbage for 5 minutes. Drain. • Peel, quarter and thinly slice the onion. Thinly slice the duck fillet. • Drain the cooked oats, reserving a little of the stock. • Mix together the warm oats and the cabbage. Pour over the oil, vinegar and Worcestershire sauce, and season to taste with pepper. Mix thoroughly. Add a little of the reserved chicken stock, if liked. • Arrange the oat salad on a serving dish and top with the onion and duck slices.

Celery and Turkey Breast Salad

The delicate flavour of celery complements the smoked turkey breast

300g/10oz celery	
2 yellow peppers	
400g/14oz smoked turkey breast	
1 small onion	
4 tbsps mayonnaise	
150ml/5fl oz natural yogurt	
2 tsps English mustard	
1 tsp maple syrup	
Salt and freshly ground white pepper	

Preparation time: 30 minutes
Nutritional value:

Analysis per serving, approx:
- 870kJ/210kcal
- 27g protein
- 7g fat
- 10g carbohydrate

Trim the celery and divide into stalks. Wash, shake dry and reserve the leaves. Wash, pat dry and slice the celery stalks. • Halve, seed, wash and thinly slice the peppers. Cut the turkey breast into matchstick strips. • Peel and grate the onion. Mix together the onion, mayonnaise, yogurt, mustard and maple syrup, and season to taste with salt and pepper. • Mix together the celery, pepper and turkey strips and stir in the mayonnaise dressing. Arrange in a serving dish and cover. Set aside to rest, at room temperature, for 10 minutes so that the flavours mingle. • Garnish with the celery leaves and serve with cracker biscuits.

Chicken Salad with Oranges

If you are very hungry, double the amount of rice

1 x 1.2 kg/2½ lb cooked chicken	
2 oranges	
2 canned pineapple rings in juice, drained	
100g/4oz cooked long-grain rice	
2 tbsps pineapple juice	
1 tbsp orange juice	
Salt	
2 egg yolks	
1 tsp Dijon mustard	
Pinch of hot paprika	
4 tbsps oil	
2 tsps chopped fresh mint	
Lettuce leaves (optional)	
Orange slices (optional)	

Preparation time: 30 minutes
Nutritional value:

Analysis per serving, approx:
- 2500kJ/600kcal
- 66g protein
- 27g fat
- 30g carbohydrate

Skin the chicken and cut the meat from the bones. Dice. • Peel the oranges, taking care to remove all the pith. Divide the oranges into segments. Quarter the segments and remove the seeds. Dice the pineapple. • Mix together the chicken, oranges, pineapple and rice. • Mix together the pineapple juice and orange juice, and season to taste with salt. Beat the egg yolks with the mustard and paprika. Gradually beat in the oil, drop by drop. Stir in the fruit juice. Pour the dressing over the chicken salad and toss lightly. • Sprinkle over the chopped mint. Garnish with the lettuce leaves and orange slices, if liked.

Delicious Poultry and Fruit Combinations

Spicy salads – light and easy to digest at the hottest time of year

Turkey Cocktail with Yogurt Sauce

Illustrated left

To serve 6:

1l/1¾ pints water
1 x 1kg/2¼ lb turkey drumstick
2 bananas
2 dessert apples
Juice ½ lemon
1 small pineapple
200g/7oz black grapes
200ml/7 fl oz double cream
450ml/15fl oz natural set yogurt
4 tsps brandy
Salt and freshly ground white pepper
6 sprigs mint

Preparation time: 1½ hours
Nutritional value:

Analysis per serving, approx:
- 2100kJ/500kcal
- 38g protein
- 20g fat
- 42g carbohydrate

Place the water in a pan and bring to the boil. Wash the drumstick, and add to the pan. Lower the heat, cover and simmer for 1 hour. • Remove from the pan and set aside to cool. • Peel the bananas, halve lengthways and slice. Quarter, peel and core the apples. Reserve a few slices for the garnish, and dice the remainder. Mix with the sliced banana, and sprinkle over the lemon juice. • Peel, halve and core the pineapple. Reserve 2 slices for the garnish, and finely dice the remainder. Wash, dry, halve and seed the grapes, reserving a few for the garnish. Add the pineapple and the remaining grapes to the apples and bananas. • Skin the turkey and cut the meat from the bone. Dice the meat and stir into the fruit salad. • Whip the cream until stiff. Stir in the yogurt and brandy, and season to taste with salt and pepper. Pour over the salad and toss lightly. • Garnish with the reserved apple slices, grapes, pineapple slices and the mint sprigs.

Oriental Chicken Salad

Illustrated right

600g/1¼ lbs skinless chicken breast fillets
25g/1oz butter
Salt and freshly ground white pepper
500g/1lb 2oz strawberries
150g/5oz bean sprouts
2 tsps diced preserved stem ginger, plus 1 tbsp of the syrup
1 tbsp basil or white wine vinegar
1 tbsp soya sauce
Pinch of cayenne
2 tbsps olive oil

Preparation time: 40 minutes
Nutritional value:

Analysis per serving, approx:
- 1200kJ/290kcal
- 37g protein
- 11g fat
- 11g carbohydrate

Wash the chicken breast fillets and pat dry. Cut the fillets into 1cm/½-inch strips. • Melt the butter, and stir-fry the chicken for 8 minutes. Season to taste with salt and pepper. Remove from the pan and drain on kitchen paper. Set aside to cool. • Wash, drain and hull the strawberries. Cut the larger fruit in half. Rinse and drain the bean sprouts. • Arrange the bean sprouts on a serving dish with the strawberries, chicken strips and diced ginger. • Mix the ginger syrup with the vinegar, soya sauce and cayenne, and season to taste with salt. Stir in the oil and pour over the salad. Toss lightly. • Cover and set aside for 10 minutes at room temperature so that the flavours mingle.

Delicious Stuffings

Apple and Chestnut Stuffing

Not only is this the traditional Christmas stuffing for turkey or goose in many families, it also tastes delicious with domestic or wild duck. The chestnuts can be replaced by stoned prunes soaked in a little dry white wine. When cooking large birds, apple and chestnut stuffing may be augmented with white bread cubes fried in butter or chopped almonds. When stuffing wild birds, the apple can be replaced by halved, seeded grapes. The amounts given are suitable for a medium-sized bird.

Peel core and slice 500g/1lb 2oz cooking apples. Place in a bowl, cover with dry red wine and set aside to marinate for about 2 hours or until the apple slices turn pink. Cut a cross in the pointed end of 500g/1lb 2oz chestnuts. Place them on a baking tray, and roast in a preheated oven at 220°C/425°F/gas mark 7 for 10 minutes.

Minced Meat Stuffing

This stuffing goes well with all poultry. The flavour can be varied with herbs and different meats as desired. When cooking very fatty birds, use lean minced veal or lamb. For less fatty birds, use mixed minced meat or minced pork. Minced meat stuffings are broken up with soaked bread or breadcrumbs and egg, mixed with the chopped giblets from the bird, herbs and seasoning.

Soak 1-2 stale slices white bread, crusts removed, in cold water. Peel and dice 3 shallots, Heat 1 tbsp vegetable oil, and fry the shallots until just beginning to colour. Squeeze out the excess water from the bread, and mix with 350-500g/11oz-1lb 2oz minced meat, 2 eggs, the shallots, 1/2 tsp salt and a pinch of ground coriander.

Bread Stuffing

This is a good choice if no substantial accompaniments are to be served with the roast; perhaps only green vegetables or salad. Bread stuffing may appear somewhat unimaginative at first glance, but it can be seasoned with the utmost subtlety and combined with unusual ingredients. For example, it may include dried fruit soaked in wine, finely chopped fresh herbs, toasted chopped almonds, raisins or sultanas, preserved stem ginger, toasted sesame seeds, as well as the diced, fried giblets from the bird.

Depending on the size of the bird, remove the crusts from 50g/2oz stale bread. Soak the bread in a light, white wine.

Buckwheat Stuffing

This satisfying, highly nutritious grain stuffing does away with the need for substantial side dishes. The stuffing may be seasoned as desired. You can also add ingredients with a distinctive flavour, such as mushrooms or wild mushrooms, garlic, a mixture of sesame and sea salt, finely chopped fresh herbs, sweetcorn, spinach, celery and onions. This stuffing can also be made from brown or wild rice, millet or pre-cooked red lentils.

Dry-fry about 250g/8oz of coarsely crushed buckwheat in a frying pan, stirring constantly, until golden.

Pour over 250ml/ 8fl oz cold water to prevent the chestnuts from drying out. Drain and allow to cool slightly. Drain the apples and reserve the marinade. Peel the chest-nuts, and mix with apple.Mix together 125ml/4 fl oz vegetable oil, a pinch of freshly ground white pepper and a pinch of paprika.

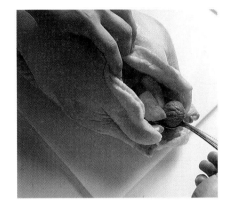

Brush the inside and outside of the bird with the flavoured oil. Rub the inside with 1/2 tsp salt. Spoon the apple and chestnut stuffing into the body cavity. Sew up the bird with trussing thread. During roasting, brush frequently with the flavoured oil and then with the reserved red wine.

Trim and finely dice the giblets. Melt 25g/1oz butter, and stir-fry for 3 minutes. Add the giblets to the minced meat, and stir in 2 tbsps snipped chives.

Rub the bird with a little salt and ground coriander. Spoon in the minced meat stuffing. Sew up with trussing thread, and roast until browned, crisp and tender.

Melt 50g/2oz butter, and stir-fry 100-150g/4-5oz diced ham, 100-150g/4-5oz thinly sliced mushrooms and the diced giblets for about 3 minutes. Squeeze out excess wine from the bread, and reserve.

Mix together the bread, 1 tsp finely chopped preserved ginger, 2 tbsps soya sauce, 2 tbsps chopped, toasted almonds, 1-2 eggs, and the mushroom mixture. Season. Spoon the stuffing into the bird. 15-30 minutes before the end of the roasting time, brush the bird with the white wine.

Trim and chop 2 celery stalks. Peel and chop 2 onions and 2 garlic cloves. Melt 25g/1oz butter, and fry the onions until transparent. Add 125-250ml/4-8fl oz dry white wine to the buckwheat, cover and cook gently for 5 minutes.

Mix the stuffing with 1 tsp finely chopped fresh thyme, 2 tbsps sesame oil and sufficient sunflower oil to make a mixture that is easy to spread. Season to taste with salt, and mix in 2 stiffly beaten egg whites.

Useful Information about Poultry and Game

Domestic Poultry

The extensive and reasonably priced range of frozen poultry was the popular choice for at least two decades. However, people nowadays are increasingly asking for fresh poultry and game. Domestic fowl includes the various weights and types of chicken, as well as partridge, duck, goose, turkey and pigeon. Poultry is highly nutritious, in terms of both density and quality. Young birds especially are low in fat and so are suitable for dieters and the health-conscious. Poultry is rich in high-quality proteins, minerals and vitamins. The fat provides valuable amounts of several unsaturated fatty acids which the body cannot produce itself and which are necessary in our daily diet. However, poultry is low in carbohydrate and fibre, which is why vegetables, pulses, potatoes, whole grains and fruit are the ideal accompaniments from a nutritional point of view.

Poultry in the Kitchen

Fresh, uncooked poultry can be stored in a bowl covered with a plate for 2 days in the refrigerator at a temperature of 2-6°C. Cooked poultry can be stored in the refrigerator for 3-4 days. Frozen poultry can be stored in the freezer or 3-star compartment of the refrigerator until its sell-by date; for 1-2 weeks in a 2-star compartment; and for a maximum of 3 days in a 1-star compartment. Frozen poultry or poultry pieces, as well as most fresh birds, are sold ready for cooking. Always remove the wrapping before defrosting. You can leave the bird in a sieve over a bowl at room temperature, but slower defrosting in the refrigerator is better. Defrosting times can vary depending on the weight. A bird weighing 1-6kg/2¼-13½lbs may take 8-30 hours to defrost at room temperature and 20-44 hours in the refrigerator.

Weight	Room temperature	Refrigerator
	hours	hours
up to 1kg/2¼lbs	8	20
1.5kg/3lbs 6oz	15	28
2kg/4½lbs	20	30
3-4kg/63/4-9lbs	24	36
5-6kg/11¼lbs-13½lbs	30	44

If a bird has to be defrosted very quickly, hold it, still frozen and in its packaging, under cold running water. This will reduce defrosting time by about 3 hours. Always discard the liquid produced during defrosting. Defrosted birds should be washed very thoroughly, inside and out, in cold running water and dried. Wash crockery and cutlery which has been in contact with the defrosting liquid in hot soapy water. Do not use a wooden board when preparing defrosted poultry. Frozen poultry tends to lose some of its individual taste. The flavour can be improved by a couple of clever tricks. One way is to rub the inside and outside of the bird with seasoned oil, cover and leave to marinate for 3-4 hours at room temperature or for 12-24 hours in the refrigerator. Corn and sunflower oil have a neutral flavour, and may be mixed with a little cayenne pepper, curry powder, ground ginger, crushed garlic or mild paprika. Alternatively, you can use dried or finely chopped fresh herbs. Those

chicken breast

chicken drumsticks

medium chicken

poussin

partridge

liver

that go particularly well with poultry are basil, tarragon, lovage, marjoram, oregano, rosemary and sage. To 125ml/4fl oz oil, use 1/2-1 tsp spice, 1 tsp dried herbs or 1 tbsp finely chopped fresh herbs. Alternatively, the bird can be left soaking in a marinade after defrosting and washing. In this case, there should be enough marinade to cover the meat completely. Otherwise it must be turned about once per hour, so that the marinade can work well into all parts of the bird. Marinating takes 6-12 hours. A poultry dish should also have a sauce, and you can use the marinade or some of it to make the sauce. Here are some examples of delicious marinades:

White wine marinade

2-3 tbsps lemon juice, 125ml/4fl oz dry white wine, 125ml/4fl oz English apple juice, pinch of sugar, freshly ground white pepper, about 10 finely chopped fresh mint leaves or 1 tsp dried mint.

Buttermilk marinade

1 chopped onion, 250ml/8fl oz buttermilk, 2 tbsps soya sauce, 1 tbsp chopped fresh root ginger, 4 tbsps white wine vinegar.

Wine and oil marinade

5 tbsps white wine vinegar, 125ml/4fl oz dry white wine, 1 chopped onion, 3 coarsely chopped garlic cloves, 6 tbsps olive oil.

When preparing fresh poultry, always check that the bird has also been fully drawn. Pluck out any remaining feathers with tweezers. Any tissues or blood residue left in the body cavity must be removed. The fat or tail gland at the rear end is also usually removed because it looks unattractive. The taste would be affected by the fat produced by the gland only in older, wild birds. If the scaly parts of the legs, head and neck are still attached to the bird, these should be cut off; some parts may be used with the giblets to make a strong poultry stock.

The cleaned giblets are usually individually wrapped and packed inside frozen birds. They must always be removed and the packaging discarded. Fresh poultry on sale in supermarkets does not include giblets, but if you buy from a butcher or poulterer, you may be able to obtain them on request.

Fresh poultry should also be thoroughly washed, both inside and outside, before cooking.

Types of Domestic Poultry

Poussin

5-6 weeks old, 250-300g/9-11oz, always oven-ready. They are used in certain speciality dishes and may also be prepared the same way as pigeon. The very small, almost fat-free chicks have no particular individual taste. 10-week old, heavier poussins are sold as coquelets and are just as tender. Poussins are often prepared with sweetbreads or veal dumplings, boned and breaded, or roast and filled with delicious stuffings, as well as served in spicy, thick sauces.

Corn-fed chicken

8-10 weeks old, 600-900g/1 1/4-2lbs, oven-ready and usually fresh rather than frozen. Corn-fed chickens have pale, delicate, almost fat-free flesh, little individual flavour and are therefore brushed with spicy sauces and grilled, breaded and fried (Viennese fried chicken in breadcrumbs) or stuffed and roasted. Poulet de Bresse, on the other hand, which is also partly fed on corn, is also allowed to range free and is especially delicious.

Medium chicken

12-16 weeks old, 1-1.4kg/2 1/4-3lbs, oven-ready and sold fresh or frozen. The giblets of frozen birds, cleaned and often individually packaged, are usually placed inside the body cavity. These chickens have already built up a thin layer of fat under the tender skin, producing a distinctive flavour as well as increased nutritional value. This layer of fat also protects the tender flesh, so that this chicken is excellent for grilling or roasting. It is also excellent for stuffing, particularly with a subtle flavour. Poaching these chickens yields a particularly

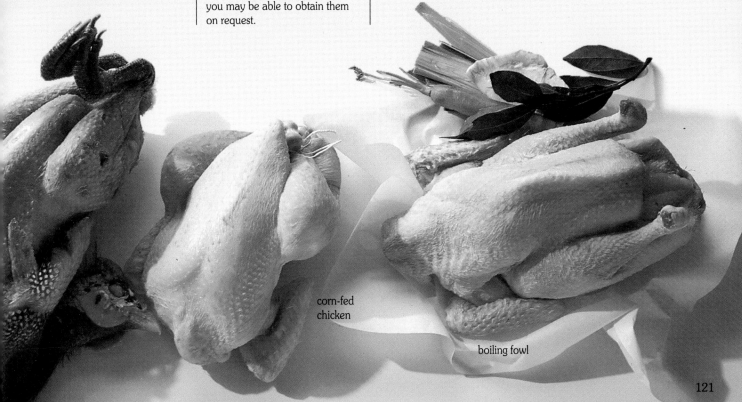

corn-fed chicken

boiling fowl

Useful Information about Poultry

delicious stock, and is the ideal way of preparing chicken for salads. Medium chickens – and corn-fed chickens – divided into portions are suitable for frying in breadcrumbs or batter, or for quick-frying or grilling in breadcrumbs.

Large and 'super' chickens
16-22 weeks old, 1.3-1.6kg/2³/₄lbs-3lbs 10oz, oven-ready, sold fresh and frozen. The giblets of frozen birds are usually supplied in the body cavity. Large and 'super' chickens have already accumulated more fat than medium chickens, but can be prepared in the same ways, as the meat is just as delicate, firm and juicy as that of smaller birds. However, the skin should be removed for those on a low-fat diet. Large chickens are also suitable for many braised dishes, where the giblets may be cooked with the bird to provide additional flavour, although they are removed before the dish is served. Chicken livers, on the other hand, are often used finely chopped in stuffings or cooked in butter to enhance sauces.

The well-known, named varieties of large chickens, such as poulards de Bresse from the Lyons region, Brussels poulards, Piemont poulards and the fatted chickens from Styria, are fattened on top-quality fodder and produce especially white, firm and tender meat.

Capon
Young, castrated cocks weighing 1.5-2kg/3lbs 6oz-4¹/₂lbs. Only rarely sold in specialist shops nowadays and used mainly in restaurant cuisine. Capons are bred for their flavoursome, tender meat and are usually sold oven-ready. They are prepared in the same ways as top-quality chickens.

Boiling fowl
Laying hens about 2 years old, 1.7-2kg/3³/₄lbs-4¹/₂lbs, usually oven-ready and fresh. Boiling fowl are better than their reputation suggests, but they are much less popular – so much less readily available – than they used to be. Although high in fat, they produce firm meat with a strong distinctive flavour. Chicken stock made with a boiling fowl has an excellent flavour. The fat can easily be removed by allowing the stock to cool and then removing the solid

layer of fat. Stock from which the fat has been removed is also used in sauces. The skin of boiling fowl is usually removed before cooking stews, braised dishes, soups and salads, as it is particularly high in fat. Boiling fowl are not suitable for roasting or grilling.

Guinea fowl
12-16 weeks old, 800g-1.2kg/1¹/₂-2¹/₂lbs, usually sold fresh only by poulterers and specialist butchers. Guinea fowl are domesticated descendants of a west African wild chicken, and, today, are primarily bred on French chicken farms. It is said that guinea fowl tastes of a combination of chicken and pheasant. Only free-range guinea fowl that are fed with special protein and corn fodder are allowed to be sold as fermiers, the finest quality. The fine flavour of guinea fowl can be brought out by subtle seasoning with bay leaf, shallots, dry white wine or thyme.

Duckling
8-10 weeks old, 1.6-1.8kg/3lbs 10oz-4lbs, oven-ready, fresh and frozen. The giblets of frozen birds are in the body cavity, individually packaged. Duckling is not very

fatty and is suitable for roasting, with or without stuffing. It may also be grilled, poached or braised. When cut into portions, it is also tasty fried.

Duck
About 1 year old, 2-2.5kg/4¹/₂lbs-5lbs 6oz, oven-ready, fresh and frozen. The individually packaged giblets of frozen birds are in the body cavity. Duck is already fatty at this age. During cooking, the fat should be skimmed off frequently. Methods of preparation are the same as for duckling.
Ducks are usually cross-bred and raised on farms in relative freedom.
Older, heavier ducks are rarely found in shops, although very occasionally they are used in braised dishes, soups and stews. Corn-fed ducks are fatty enough to be preserved as confit in their own fat. The famous Rouen duck is a particularly heavy breed weighing about 3kg/6³/₄lbs. It is

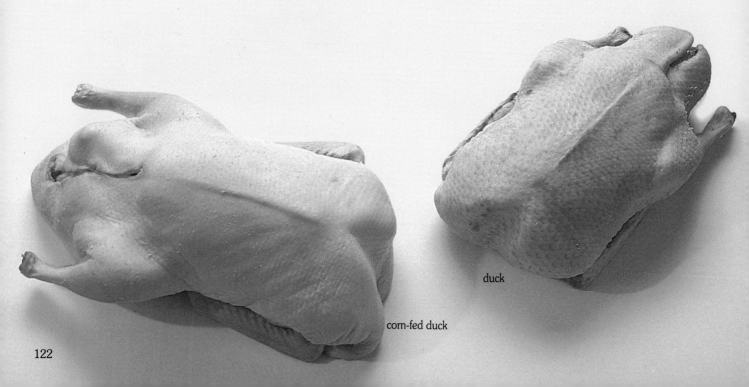

duck

corn-fed duck

smothered rather than slaughtered in the usual way, so that the blood remains in the body. Rouen duck is always roasted at a very high temperature for a very short time. Duck acquires a pleasant flavour if filled with red or white wine the evening before cooking. To do this, pull the neck skin tightly under the abdomen and secure. Pink roast duck breast, which is in frequent demand nowadays, has skin which usually stays pale and soft as a result of the short roasting times. The skin is therefore removed from each slice of duck breast and individually roasted until brown and crispy. Then, the skin is replaced around the breast slices, cut into pieces if necessary.

Young goose

3-5 months old, about 4kg/9lbs oven-ready, fresh and sometimes frozen. The giblets of frozen birds are individually packaged inside the body cavity. Geese up to 5 months old are still in their first plumage, have a flexible breastbone and are less fatty than older birds. Nevertheless, a bird weighing about 4kg/9lbs will lose 500-600g/1lb 2oz-1$\frac{1}{2}$lbs in fat.

Goose

Young goose, 7-10 months old, 5-6kg/11$\frac{1}{4}$-13$\frac{1}{2}$lbs. Geese are sold frozen and fresh, usually oven-ready. The neck and giblets of frozen birds are individually packaged inside the body cavity. The meat of free-range geese yields the much-loved typical taste, as they live outdoors from spring until late autumn, feed on soft foliage, in addition to corn, and thus develop extremely well. Fattening begins only shortly before slaughter. Geese fattened on oats are especially sought-after, since the oats also enhance the flavour.

Geese over 1 year old are no longer suitable for roasting because the meat is rather tough. They should be braised, or the cooked meat can be used in stuffings. Older geese may be recognized by their highly brittle bones and their slightly dark yellow fat.

Fatty geese or ducks lose a lot of fat before roasting if they are steamed. The oven-ready bird should first be pricked evenly all over with a darning needle, so that the fat can escape. However, take care to pierce only the layer of fat, not the meat itself. Place the bird in a steamer over vigorously

boiling water and steam, tightly covered, for 15-40 minutes, depending on size and fat content. Then roast the bird as desired, but for a slightly shorter time than usual.

Turkey

Originating in Central America, the turkey is only rarely found in the wild today. Turkeys are bred commercially on special farms, subject to stringent regulations. These ensure a fairly homogenous quality for turkeys and all turkey pieces. Rearing involves three fattening phases, as follows.

Baby turkey

9-11 weeks old, 2-3kg/4$\frac{1}{2}$-6$\frac{3}{4}$lbs, mainly sold frozen, but also fresh. The neck and giblets of frozen birds are individually packaged inside the body cavity. Baby turkeys are extremely popular because their meat is especially tender and they can easily be roasted whole, with or without stuffing.

Young turkey

After the second fattening phase, at 12-16 weeks, they weigh 3-5kg/6$\frac{3}{4}$-11$\frac{1}{4}$lbs. They are sold fresh and frozen. The giblets of

frozen birds are individually packaged inside the body cavity. The cartilaginous joints of young turkeys are still flexible and not yet brittle. The meat is more flavoursome and juicier than that of baby turkey and is slightly fattier.

Turkey

Turkeys have completed the third fattening phase and reached an oven-ready weight of 5-8kg/11$\frac{1}{4}$-18lbs or more. The popular turkey pieces from which such a wide variety of meals can be made are provided by these heavy birds, as well as large young turkeys. The pieces are sold both frozen and as fresh poultry.

Poultry cuts

Chicken, duck, turkey and even goose are also sold as cuts. This makes it easier to enjoy poultry and game birds if your household contains only one or two people, as pieces can be used in meals which do not require a whole bird.

Poultry pieces and giblets

These are principally used to make stocks or soups and as the basis of fine sauces. Poultry offal is

goose

turkey

Useful Information about Poultry

usually sold frozen. In theory, the meat could be cooked from frozen, as only the extract is required. However, for reasons of hygiene, we recommended defrosting offal in a sieve, discarding the liquid and thoroughly washing the meat before cooking.

Liver

Sold both fresh and frozen. Frozen liver should be defrosted. Carefully remove any remaining fat from each liver, wash, pat dry and use as described in individual recipes.

Gizzard

Used in stuffings and, with the offal, for poultry stock. The gizzard should be thoroughly washed and then cooked according to the recipe. For stuffings, the dark red flesh is separated from the hard grey skin.

Heart

Also sold fresh or frozen. Frozen heart should be defrosted. All blood residue and remaining skin must be meticulously removed and the heart thoroughly washed. Preparing a dish from chicken heart is quite time-consuming because the hearts are very small.

It is better to use goose or turkey hearts. However, chicken hearts are the only part of poultry and game birds which are entirely free of cholesterol.

Drumsticks

These provide satisfying and tasty meals. Chicken drumsticks weigh about 165g/6oz, duck drumsticks about 200g/7oz, goose drumsticks 350-500g/11oz-1lb 2oz, and turkey drumsticks about 1kg/2¼ lbs. Turkey drumsticks are usually separated and sold as thighs and legs. A thigh weighs about 700g/1lb 6oz and the leg about 300g/10oz. In addition, turkey wings are also sold individually; one wing weighs about 300g/10oz.

Breast

To many people, the breasts of poultry are the best parts, and usually contain the least fat. Turkey breast is sold as escalopes of about 150g/5oz, or rolled into portions of 300-800g/10oz-1½ lbs. Goose breasts weigh about 700g/1lb 6oz. Smoked goose breast is a delicacy and weighs 350-400g/11-14oz. Whole chicken breasts weigh about 220g/7½ oz; skinned fillets weigh about 150g/5oz.

Wild Poultry and Game Birds

Nowadays, the most popular game birds are pheasant, partridge, grouse, quail, wild duck and wild pigeon. In some countries, however, thrushes, woodcock and wild geese are still shot, but in most of Europe, these birds are officially protected. Even pheasant, grouse and quail have little chance of breeding in the wild because the right environment is no longer available and food sources are increasingly under threat. Game birds are, therefore, generally raised on private estates.

Wild game birds are leaner than domestic poultry and game. Young birds provide tender meat which is excellent for roasting. The tougher meat of older birds should be braised to tenderize it. Above all, wild game birds have a particular piquant flavour which increases if the bird is hung, still in its plumage. Modern taste is for birds to be hung for a shorter time than used to be the case in the past. Today, 24-48 hours is regarded as sufficient to bring out the special delicious flavour. Exceptions to this are quail and wild duck, which should not be hung, but prepared immediately after shooting.

Young wild birds should be roasted until the meat is pale pink and juicy. The tender, low-fat meat of game birds can be covered in bacon slices. Small birds can be wrapped entirely in bacon, a process called larding. Fatty, unsmoked, fresh bacon is best for larding. Remove the bacon just before the end of the cooking time so that the skin can brown. If you also want to eat the bacon for its flavour, smoked bacon is better, but remember to use less salt when seasoning the bird as the bacon also contains salt. Game birds are usually stuffed in the same way as domestic poultry; the body cavity openings are sewn up or pinned together and the bird is also trussed as required.

If you are uncertain about the age of a bird, it is safer to braise it. An old bird can be marinated for 2-3 days beforehand. A marinade made from white wine, light wine vinegar, cloves, diced onion or shallot and ½ a bay leaf is especially good for this. When preparing braised dishes, the sauce can be flavoured with some of the marinade.

pheasant

domestic pigeon

Domestic pigeon/wild pigeon

Young birds are 6-10 weeks old, 300-400g/10-14oz, and are not widely on sale. Only young birds are suitable for roasting or grilling, either with or without stuffing. Young birds have pale, beige feet (older birds have darker, brownish grey feet), a relatively thick beak and some remaining down feathers on the breast. However, since young pigeons are also sold oven-ready (previously plucked), a young bird can best be identified by its flexible breastbone; this is hard and stiff in older pigeons. Domestic pigeons, that is, those bred for consumption, have a finer, milder flavour than wild pigeons. Older pigeons can be used for braised dishes, soups and stuffings. Young pigeons should be larded for roasting or grilling to stop the meat drying out. Pigeons are only sold fresh, never frozen.

Pheasant

Breeding cock pheasants weigh about 1kg/2¼lbs, and hens up to about 900g/2lbs. In the wild, cocks reach a weight of 1.3kg/2¾lbs, and hens 1kg/2¼lbs. Pheasant is one of the most frequently hunted wild birds. Pheasant cocks less than 1 year old can be identified by the truncated, conical spur on the back of the leg. This spur is pointed in older cocks. Hens less than 1 year old have a wart-like projection instead of a spur, which becomes longer and spur-like in older hens. Young pheasants have a soft breastbone. Pheasants are sold fresh and oven-ready, as well as in their plumage. Young pheasants are suitable for roasting, with or without stuffing; older pheasants are mainly suitable for braising or making into dumplings, mousses or pies. The fine, aromatic individual flavour of pheasant should never be drowned by strong flavourings or the excessive use of one spice.

Partridge

Partridges weigh 100-400g/4-14oz. They are drawn immediately and then hung in their plumage. Only young partridges are suitable for roasting. Young partridges can be recognized by their yellow to pale brown legs, jet-black beak and pointed outer wing feathers. In addition, the tip of the breastbone of young partridges is still flexible and the plumage does not yet have the white breastplate of partridges after their autumn moulting. Older birds can be identified by their dark brown legs, pale beak and rounded wing tips. Partridges are always sold fresh, but are not very often available. Young partridges are roasted. Older birds are braised and should be marinated in a white wine marinade for 2 days beforehand.

Grouse

The grouse is particularly highly prized in Britain, and the red or Scotch grouse, which is found only in the British Isles, is considered the best. Other varieties include the black grouse and the capercaillie. Young birds can be recognized by the downy feathers on the breast and under the wings, and the rich brown feathers on the head and neck. Grouse is sold fresh. Young birds have the best flavour and may be roasted. They should be larded with bacon as the flesh is inclined to be dry. Older birds maybe braised or cooked in a pie.

Quail

Quails weigh 100-200g/4-7oz. Only breeding quails are heavier than this. They are the smallest and most delicious of all wild birds. Most commercially sold quails are no longer caught in the wild, but come from farms. This means they can be slaughtered when they are at the best age for consumption, that is, when they have accumulated a suitably thick layer of fat. Young quails have pale yellow legs. Quails are always sold oven-ready, often even pre-roasted or prepared in some other way, or stuffed. Fresh quails should be bought ready plucked so that the fattiest birds can be selected. As quails have a natural layer of fat under the skin, they do not necessarily have to be larded.

Wild duck

Depending on species and age, wild ducks weigh 1-2kg/2¼-4½lbs. However, in this part of the world, those shot are mainly mallards. The drake weighs 1.2-1.5kg/2½lbs-3lbs 6oz; the duck 750g-1kg/1½-2¼lbs. Young wild ducks can be identified by the ease with which the webs on their feet can be removed. Young wild ducks are roasted pink; older birds are braised after marinating.

quails

partridges

Index